Flashbacks in Post-Traumatic Stress Disorder: Surviving the Flood

Copyright © 2012 Leslie Raddatz

Cover jacket designed, conceived and illustrated © 2012
Bonnie Toews, Whistler House, Canada.

Image © Getty Images

Interior design © 2012 by Moonlight Spirit Publications

Edited © 2012 by Janell Moon and Leslie Raddatz

Library of Congress Cataloguing-in-Publication Data

All rights reserved. No part of this book may be reproduced in any form without permission in writing from the publisher.
Moonlight Spirit Publications
PO Box 2452, Oshkosh, WI 54903

Raddatz, Leslie

Flashbacks in Post-Traumatic Stress Disorder: Surviving the Flood

A healing and inspiring memoir

ISBN-13: 978-1475224085
ISBN-10: 1475224087
LCCN: 2012907712

Flashbacks in Post-Traumatic Stress Disorder: Surviving the Flood

A Healing and Inspiring Memoir

Leslie M Raddatz

Dedication

This book is dedicated to all the children, teenagers, and adults that suffer with abusive relationships and/or memories.

To those who suffer with Post-Traumatic Stress Disorder and other mental illnesses that are present because of the abuse and trauma endured.

Dedicated to all our women and men veterans and their families affected by mental illness.

In honor of my father's memory—a Vietnam veteran that suffered with PTSD.

Who was blown out of a supply truck, received a Purple Heart and an honorable discharge.

My father's message to veterans:

"Get counseling immediately after you come home from war so you can talk about what you experienced during combat and the loss of friends. Please keep yourself and your family safe.

Keep all of your records so you can prove your service to our country. If your disability is denied, keep trying to overturn the decision. It took 30 years of patience and a lot of paperwork to finally receive 80% of my disability benefits."

My father passed away from kidney cancer along with tumors in several areas. He fought his cancer for seven years while he kept trying for a 100% disability from the army.

Contents

Acknowledgements ix
Introduction xv

Part One: Trauma and Abuse
Chapter 1: Family Secret 3
Chapter 2: New Beginnings 11
Chapter 3: Tears Start to Fall 15
Chapter 4: Family History 25
Chapter 5: Pebbles Thrown into the Water 41
Chapter 6: Three Secrets 47
Chapter 7: Blinded by the Flood Light 59

Part Two: Abuse Turned Inward
Chapter 8: Submerged in Water 75

Part Three: Unconditional Love
Chapter 9: Life Preserver 83
Chapter 10: A Child Was Born 95

Part Four: Ex-husband's Abuse Surfaces
Chapter 11: Swim to the Surface 103

Part Five: Darkness into the Light
Chapter 12: God's Love 113

Part Six: Admission to a Psychiatric Unit
Chapter 13: Out of Control Crisis Care 119
Chapter 14: Being Honest with Myself 131
Chapter 15: Trusting Myself 141
Chapter 16: Home Sweet Home 157

Part Seven: Healing Continues
Chapter 17: Affects on Family Relationships   165
Chapter 18: The Psychiatrist   173
Chapter 19: Art and Attachment Therapy   189
Chapter 20: Complete Resolution   211

Part Eight: How I Survived the Flood
Chapter 21: Life After the Flood   227

Part Nine: Author Letter to Readers
Chapter 22: Letter from the Author   237

Testimonials   241

About The Author   251

Acknowledgements

Lisa thank you for being a fellow survivor that read my manuscript and wrote my first testimonial. This gave me confidence that my book will be helpful and inspiring to other readers.

Natalie thank you for your photography expertise to help represent my story clearly through photos on my platforms.

Emily thank you for being the coworker who supported me throughout my healing process, especially the emergency stage. I also thank you for giving me the courage to write this book and for the assurance that my story was worth telling. Your belief that I owed it to the people to inspire them throughout their healing journey helped me.

My husband thank you for being my true love and friend. You taught me that everything is possible when you have the right partner. You helped me through earning my two bachelor degrees, the birth of our son, struggles with our teenage daughters, and my entire healing process. You have really shown me that you are here to stay and that you love me unconditionally. I love you!

My daughters thank you for your patience, love and understanding while I was struggling emotionally. We have had to share some difficulties and weather some storms but I think we have done alright. I love you and wish you wonderful things for your future.

My son, five years old, thank you for your love and innocence as you show mommy how much fun it is to play. I enjoy when you share how your day went, what you learned at daycare and the exciting adventures you experience on your fieldtrips.

My sister, Pam, for helping me to see I was worth loving and not to settle for an abusive relationship when a healthy one was waiting for me to discover it. You also taught me how to fight for what I want in my life instead of waiting for it to happen on its own. You were there to hold me when I cried in every step of my healing process. You had the strength to admit wrong doing when you were a child. Without you I don't think I would have made it through the emergency stage of the healing process.

My sister, Kim, for helping me my entire life. As a young child you were my first responsible mother figure who took care of me as well as you could at the age of six. You have always been there for me with no judgment. You listened and offered your gentle advice and taught me not to worry about what people thought of me. You told me everyone's journey is unique and that no one knows the struggles in your life.

Bill—thank you for being a compassionate and loving friend. You offered your advice and shared personal information about your traumas and gave me hope that the emergency stage wouldn't last for long. When I was in the hospital, you called me several times to check on my progress. I want you to know how much your friendship means to me.

My sister, Sonya, for showing me that you could become a successful woman in New York, despite our upbringing. I always admired you and strived to be like you by reaching my personal best. You were there when I needed to talk, you listened, and when I needed advice you gave it without the sugar coating. I enjoy my annual trips to New York to experience new and happy memories with just the two of us.

My mom and dad for helping me through the healing process when I came to you with difficult questions and wanting to know why you did or didn't do certain things in my childhood. You were open and explained your struggles as you began your own healing process from the personal challenges in your lives. You never gave up and in my adulthood you really became good friends to me because you were able to stop denying the past. Thank you mom and dad, I think I know how painful it must have been.

Eddie—for always being funny in childhood when we needed a laugh to take our minds off our abusive homes. I will never forget the robot performance to the "Who's Johnny" song or sharing in the fear as we watched "creature feature" on television. Also thanks for the many trips to the cookie jar you made for our sugar enjoyment.

Sandy—thank you for helping me through the most difficult part of my life, which was reprocessing the traumatic and abusive memories. You helped me recognize triggers, taught me coping skills and really spent time to get to know and help me. You became more than a therapist to me. I think of you as a friend that I can trust with anything. Thank you for changing my life and helping me reach freedom from PTSD, conversion and somatization disorders.

Kathy—thank you for helping me cope with my trauma and memories through the use of art therapy. It feels good to be able to create something positive out of something so negative. I enjoy our time of counsel, creation and reflection. We have come to really know each other and I count you, as a very good friend. Thank you for changing my perspective about being able to do art. I always thought of myself as someone that wasn't good enough so I never attempted it. You showed me that anyone can and should experience art at his or her level of personal ability. I will take what I learned and utilize it throughout the rest of my life.

Dr. Peterson for having the answers and knowing the combination of medications to prescribe to help me reclaim my life. Also, for the encouraging talks about it being possible to live a normal life while I was learning how to cope with my disorders.

Janell Moon, author of twelve non-fiction books and my editor, writing coach and encourager, when I felt discouraged. You were my rock as I went through the long rewrite and editing process. Thank you for reassuring me that it would be worth all the hard work in the end.

Barbara Shelton- who has become a dear friend and fellow advocate for people with PTSD. Thank you so much Barbara for the wonderful five-day interview you posted on your blog. Meeting you has truly made a difference in my life.

Blair Corbett—Founder and Executive Director of *Ark of Hope* for Children, Inc. who asked me to help abused victims by being a facilitator on the Justice for All Revolution website. Thank you Blair for having the confidence in me to help others while making a difference in their lives.

Ella Sandwell—author of *Goodbye Martha*, thank you for having me on your radio show and helping me advertise my book as well as creating awareness on the subjects of PTSD, conversion and somatization disorders. You have been a real blessing.

Bonnie Toews, Author of *The Consummate Traitor*, thank you for reaching out to me and taking interest in publishing my articles about my father's Vietnam experiences and his struggles at the end of his life. I also thank you for writing my back cover description, designing my book jacket, looking over my proposal, and giving me helpful tips. You were the first one to help me in my book publishing journey and also giving me some publishing credits. You have become a really good friend.

Thank you for all the prayer support of my parish and religious community.

These people acknowledged are proof that God's guidance brought all them into my life to help me get published. Without all of these people there would be no book. I needed a lot of support while writing this book because I wrote it while in crisis mode and that is why I was able to capture every appointment, every memory, every feeling, every tear and happy memories as well.

Thank you to everyone who helps my book get into the right hands so healing can begin.

Introduction

This book *Flashbacks in Post-Traumatic Stress Disorder: Surviving the Flood* is about a courageous journey of a little girl who struggles to survive sexual, physical, and emotional abuse because of parental neglect and lack of supervision. It will take you through her process of healing.

This book was written to inspire other victims, survivors, and loved ones of post-traumatic stress disorder as well as other mental illnesses that they can do better. I illustrate how post-traumatic stress disorder, conversion, and somatization disorders began taking over my life. I was unaware of what was occurring as I attempted to keep my suffering with panic attacks, zoning out, disassociating, nervousness, paranoia, and flashbacks with body memories a secret for eleven years. Terrified that I was losing my mind, I didn't receive the help I needed and it affected the way I treated my family.

I am confident if I had a book like this detailing my disorders, I would have received help earlier and it may have saved me from admittance into the hospital for crisis care.

I was fortunate to have a wonderful therapist who knew exactly which therapies to recommend for PTSD, conversion and somatization disorders: attachment therapy, EMDR, Brainspotting, resource building, and positive imagery. She also taught me how to set boundaries and many coping skills to help when I was triggered.

I also had a wonderful art therapist that balanced trauma work with fun for my "child within." Art therapy reached the "child within" through play and ultimately gained the child's trust, love, and acceptance. This helped me to understand that the adult self loved her and would protect her. This also assisted with trauma work because the "child within" would share more as she became more comfortable and felt secure to talk about the abuse and trauma she experienced. My art therapist used playful imagery to help connect my "child within" with my adult self.

After the hospital stay, I was able to find a knowledgeable psychiatrist. He was very important in my healing journey because he was the first person in eleven years to have the answers. He explained my disorders and why the symptoms were occurring and also how to stabilize them. Before I met my psychiatrist, my PTSD, conversion and somatization symptoms affected my entire life to the point of being in the flight or fight mode most of the time. This meant I was always waiting for the next threat that never came. My body didn't recognize that my trauma and abuse happened in the past so it was waiting for the next attack and all my time and energy was used to survive from day-to-day.

It affected my family because all my energy and attention was focused on survival. My daughters would do something as simple as hug me without asking permission or by scaring me with a joke and it put me immediately into crisis mode. My psychiatrist was able to prescribe the right combination of medications and today, I am thriving and happy with my life. My children are also happy to have their fun and loving mom back. My husband and I can finally relax and spend quality time together. There are still many things to work on because PTSD never goes away but now I have the tools to quickly address the triggers so I can return to a relaxed state quickly without interruption of my daily activities.

I look forward to my therapy sessions and my visits to my psychiatrist's office because the fear and the unknown are gone. I want to educate readers so they too can feel relaxed and know what to expect when they start their healing journey.

I also met along my healing journey Janell Moon who is a bestselling author of nonfiction books, counselor and writing coach. She was also a big part of my healing process because she helped me write my story and reach my goals to help others. She educated me about what writing techniques to use to successfully convey my message to my intended readers.

This book is to:
- Help educate others about sexual abuse, trauma, and help them to recognize the patterns and warning signs. I also want to help validate someone who is experiencing similar feelings or illnesses and are frightened but don't understand what is occurring.

- This book is also about not repeating the patterns of abuse and to heal and reclaim life. It is important to teach children how to protect themselves as they grow into adolescence and adulthood.

Flashbacks in Post-Traumatic Stress Disorder: Surviving the Flood will demonstrate what freedom and success means through my eyes.

Freedom:
- from another person's control
- from those who abuse you
- from abuse including self sabotage
- from judgment of others
- from insults that cut deep into your soul
- from silence—no more secrets
- from self doubt
- from the haunting memories—flashbacks & body memories
- from feeling blamed or at fault
- to live without anxiety, depression, or panic

Success:
- independence from co-dependency
- free the abused "child within"

- learning how to love that hurt child and help integrate with the adult
- learning that you are worth putting yourself first
- feeling worthy of love and self worth
- positive self image
- facing your fears with courage
- feeling confident and strong
- accomplish achievements that were once out of your reach

If you are reading this book, you will experience how I personally broke through the trauma and abuse, found freedom, and how I reached the many successes once I made up my mind that I was worth it.

Author note to readers:

When you see text in italics throughout the book, it means I am experiencing a flashback or I reverted back to feelings of a child while in therapy treatment sessions: EMDR, brainspotting, ego-state, and attachment therapy, etc. I also experience the flashbacks on my own at home and throughout my everyday life activities. I am unable to separate past from present until the traumatic memories are reprocessed so the writing in italics is in present tense. In this state of mind, I am frightened and in a fight or flight mode to survive.

This book details the memories that were recalled after being repressed for 32 years while under a professional therapist's care. All of the names and some details were changed to protect the identity of the people involved.

Part One
Trauma and Abuse

Chapter 1
Family Secret

I am younger than five years old and remember being in my grandmother's kitchen watching her wash the dishes. I am eating a gigantic moist chocolate brownie and a large glass of white milk. I hear my mother yell from the living room the dreaded words, "Kids, it's time to go home!" This means it is time to say good-bye to Great Uncle Charlie. I begin to panic and know what I have to do.

I give my grandmother a long hug good-bye soaking up her safety and love, not wanting to let go of her damp apron. Then I slowly walk towards the living room. I stop at the threshold of where the kitchen ends and the hallway begins. I look behind me one last time while inhaling and exhaling, as my grandmother says with her trusting voice, "Go ahead, Tweetie, say good-bye to your Great Uncle Charlie."

I continue cautiously down the hallway noticing the sand on the cement flooring as I hear the grainy sand make noise as I shuffle my feet. I reach Great Uncle Charlie's room half way down the hall and briefly peer in, noticing he's not in his room. I take another deep breath as I continue towards the living room. I arrive in the doorway, observing my mother and father visiting with Great Uncle Charlie. Their visit is shortened as they notice my arrival. They both say with reassuring voices, "Go ahead, give your Great Uncle Charlie a hug and kiss goodbye," as they both leave the room to say good-bye to my grandmother and to locate my other three sisters.

As I slowly approach my uncle, sitting in his lazy chair, I feel sick inside and my intuition tells me to run. When I get close enough for him to grab me, he abruptly yanks my arm and starts his long good-bye that I think wouldn't end. He presses his body next to mine to the point where we are one body, rubbing his chest against mine, then patting the front of my chest, where my undeveloped breasts are. He makes a "Woo Woo" sound over and over again in my ear. Then he rubs his beard stubble against my face until it is red, raw, and burning, then the kissing starts with his sloppy saliva wet on my mouth.

I try to be a good girl and listen to my parents. When I can't stand it anymore, I struggle to separate from his hold. As I am thrown backwards, I look at his face of complete satisfaction. I feel sick and hurt by the adults who gave me any sense of safety.

Then I witness my three sisters Sonya, Victoria and Andie's pain as I watch the same thing happen to them. When we are all done with our good-byes, I get in the car feeling dirty and confused.

As I flash back to the present, I hear a car horn honking at me. The light is green. I say defensively, "Okay, I am going! Give me a minute!" I continue to drive to work as I flash back again to the past:

Victoria and I go to the kitchen to get some food. I struggle to open the heavy refrigerator and when it is finally open I see with disappointment and anxiety that there is no food. Victoria quickly gets a chair and opens the cupboards and reports they are empty. My stomach feels sick as I know we have to go to grandma's house to spend time with Great Uncle Charlie again.

My grandmother is happy to see us as we enter the front door, promptly at noon. She asks, "Did you have lunch yet?" We shake our heads, while she begins to make us lunch. We visit happily as grandma sits down and joins us. We eat slowly enjoying every moment but then after lunch grandma says, "Go outside and play with Uncle Charlie." Victoria and I glance sadly at each other and know that is what we have to do to show our appreciation.

Our Great Uncle Charlie is already waiting for us at the door. We take a big ball and start taking turns bouncing it to each other, then to Great Uncle Charlie.

Flashbacks in Post-Traumatic Stress Disorder: Surviving the Flood

He returns the ball to one of us and the cycle continues. As our play progresses, I see a look of anger in my sister's face as she bounces the ball too high towards my uncle. He struggles to maintain his balance while he returns the ball to us. I understand the anger my sister feels and I follow her lead.

As our anger is unleashed and no longer contained, we continue to bounce the ball too high, out of his reach and the speed starts to spiral out of control with every turn. As we watch him struggle to keep the ball and himself in control, we feel powerful for once.

The feeling of control was replaced with panic, remorse, and anxiety as we see him lose his balance and goes crashing to the ground. We both went to his side begging for forgiveness, reassuring him we didn't mean to hurt him. As my sister stands up and instructs me to stay with him, he has a look of joy and satisfaction, while she runs for help.

When my sister returns with my grandmother, we witness the love and concern she has for her twin. She looks at both of us and asks, "What happened?" I stand there frozen in place as my sister takes all the blame. I feel guilty as my grandmother looks at her with disappointment and anger.

We watch my grandmother hurry to get the car as he lay motionless on the ground. She struggles to help him into the car, as he stares at us, groaning with pain.

As she drives away, we feel sorry for what we did and worry about what is wrong. When the car disappears into the distance, we knock on her neighbor's door and ask to stay for a while. We hang our heads down in shame as we explain what happened.

A long time passes before my grandmother returns and explains to her neighbor the consequences of our actions. He has a broken hip and will need her assis-

tance for a while. Then she turns to us and says, "Let's go!" In the car ride home, we are quiet and it is never spoken about again.

I am half way to work as I just become alert and notice I am going over the bridge but didn't remember leaving the stop light. I shake it off as I say to myself you are just sleepy from the morning, as I zone out again:

My sisters seem to take all their frustrations out on me. It is so easy because I am the youngest and the weakest. My sister, Sonya, is fighting with me in the dining room. Then she punches me in the stomach and it knocks the wind out of me. I scream and cry as my mother comes to break up the fight. I run to my bedroom as I did many times before isolating myself from my family.

Later that night, Victoria and Sonya, talks about Sonya's boyfriend problems. Victoria was tired and decides to go to bed. When she wakes up, she sees Sonya on the floor crawling toward her and in a raspy voice repeating "Help, Help!" As I am sleeping, I awake to a desperate call for help coming from Victoria's bedroom, which is right beside my room. She shouts, "Sonya did something stupid!" As I stand in the doorway, I see Sonya on the floor, barely able to talk. My dad rushes upstairs while Victoria is screaming at Sonya telling her to "Tell dad what you did!" As she tries to talk, her voice is quiet and raspy as she confesses that she took pills. In a panic, my dad scoops Sonya up in his arms and yells to my mom. "I'm taking Sonya to the hospital!"

My dad is backing the car out of the driveway as I ask my mother, "You don't think it is because we fought earlier do you?" There was no response from my mother so I assume all the responsibility. As panic sets in I ask, "Is she going to die because of me?" I hear no response; receive no comfort or reassurance that she will be all right. As my mom gets into the car, I watch as my parents drive away. I pray she wouldn't die because of the hurtful words I said to her during our fight. Victoria and I stay home waiting for news on Sonya's condition.

Flashbacks in Post-Traumatic Stress Disorder: Surviving the Flood

The doctors' pump her stomach to remove the poison. I am so relieved to get the news that she is going to be okay. She is admitted to the hospital on the unit where they keep the patients who are in need of protection.

The question of why she did it is a mystery to everyone but me. I know it is because I told her I hate her and that she isn't my sister anymore. To my surprise that isn't the reason. My family is asked to participate in a counseling session where Sonya can speak and my parents have to listen. I remember entering the room and sitting in a circle of chairs with my sisters and my parents.

The discussion is open for Sonya to talk about why she tried to take her life. I feel she is testing the waters as she speaks about not having enough food and what we have to resort to when the toilet paper and pads run out. My parents deny it completely. Then she speaks of my Great Uncle Charlie's sexual abuse and again my parents are not supportive. My father's response is anger saying, "He never touched me as a boy and I grew up around him." I sit there listening and feel relief that it wasn't my fault.

My other two sisters, Victoria and Andie, are asked if they are happy at home. Then I am asked. I said, "Yes," even though I wasn't but the fear of going to a foster home petrified me. I heard scary stories of abuse in foster homes so I make the decision to stay where I am because I knew what to expect. I think my other two sisters answered the same way because Sonya is the only one going to a foster home. We are unable to see her for a while but in a short time she returns home to live.

I am almost to work but notice I went the wrong way. I have to back track to get back on the right road. I am frustrated at myself as I tell myself I have to get more sleep at night.

I am preparing for my eighth grade graduation. It is a very important day for me. I am so happy that I completed middle school. I am wearing my dark blue dress with pink flowers. I put my makeup on and fix my hair and remember feeling pretty as I look at myself in the mirror.

When it comes time to go down to the gymnasium, I know my dad is there to watch me graduate and my mom is at home fixing the food for my graduation party.

My stomach has butterflies in it as I walk down the aisle with confidence to receive my certificate and wait to hear my name announced. As I hear my name, I feel the tears of joy in my eyes and a feeling of accomplishment in my heart. When the ceremony is over, I quickly find my dad so we can walk home to my party.

When I walk into the front door everyone yells "Happy graduation!" I stand for a moment to enjoy the streamers, balloons and the faces of happy people who are there to see and congratulate me. I feel so much love in the room that I was overflowing with joy.

My mom is so proud of the feast she prepared for my family and friends. I am so grateful because I know how much money this must have cost. She tells everyone to help themselves as she shows me my special cake, Tweetie bird with a graduation cap with the frosting being in bright cheerful colors. The words "Happy Graduation, Tweetie" makes me laugh because even though I am older, I still allow my family to call me by my childhood nickname.

Everyone is eating and talking. I stop by each cluster of people to thank them for coming and reminisced with them about the humorous Tweetie they knew.

The day couldn't get happier than this and I remember sitting on the sofa tired with my shoes off and on the foot stool. I didn't want this day to end. Then there is a knock at the door. While the door slowly opens and the faces are revealed it is my Uncle Tom with my Aunt Violet and they brought my Great Uncle Charlie. I haven't seen them for two years since my grandmother died. I am upset that my Great Uncle Charlie is at my graduation.

My mother greets them as they walk through the front door. I take a deep breath and put my happy face on when I hear my mother yell, "Give your Great Uncle Charlie a hug." My aunt Violet helps my Great Uncle Charlie to the sofa and he sits down. I have many emotions going through my body. I didn't want to hug him. My intuition surfaces and tells me to run away. I ignore it because I can't be rude. I listen to my mother and do what she told me.

I lean into give him a hug and he pulls me close as he is hugging me and rubbing his beard stubble on my face. He places his hands on my small breasts squeezing them while making the "Woo Woo" sound in my ear. I pull away from him and look around the room in shock that no one witnessed what just happened. Everyone was engaged in conversation and again I feel let down that I wasn't protected. I run out the front door and sit on the steps and begin to cry. I can't stop my thoughts from asking the questions: Did my grandmother know that her twin brother was abusing her four grandchildren? If she did, why didn't she stop him? Then the thought enters my mind that maybe it is a sick secret the whole family knows about but does nothing to stop it? As I calm myself down, I prepare to go back into the house with the happy face everyone expects to see.

To avoid having to say good-bye to my Great Uncle Charlie, I go upstairs to my bedroom to be alone. I said good-bye to my family and the few friends that are still visiting. I thank my parents for the wonderful party and said, "I am tired and need to go to bed." As I walk up the stairs backwards, I see my Great Uncle Charlie disappear with each step. I vow to myself to never see him again.

The car is parked. I am confused as I sit there wondering how I arrived at work. I am in a daze as I remember:

My dad receives the call that my Great Uncle Charlie died. My sisters refuse to go to the funeral and they are all adults by this time. I am in high school and my father depends solely on me to go with him.

I need my dad's acceptance and attention so I go with him. As I walk into the funeral home, soft music is playing in the background as my family greets us and thanks us for coming. I try to ignore the family members who are slandering my sisters for not coming. They talk of the untrue accusations my sisters made about poor Great Uncle Charlie. I feel frozen in place not able to move or say a word. As I scan the room, everyone is mourning this monster that hurt small children and no one seems to know the truth but me. I feel like screaming from the rooftops how he sexually abused all of us girls but I have no courage to do this. Everyone in this small town pitied him for being almost blind and the fact he never married. I am sick to my stomach and furious with myself because I didn't speak up or defend my sisters' honor. I feel like a coward, a trader, and an imposter.

When it is my turn to go up to pay my respects, I look at his motionless body and start to sob uncontrollably. I can only imagine everyone who sees me assumes it is sadness for the loss of my Great Uncle Charlie and shock because they didn't know we were so close. It wasn't that at all. It was the feeling of freedom I felt happy knowing I would never be forced to say good-bye to him again. As I bow my head, I pray to God to first judge him harshly and then mercy for his soul. It is very quiet on the way home as my dad mourns the loss of his uncle and I am relieved by his death.

I go inside work, set my things down and decided that it was time to seek professional help because the flashbacks, dizzy spells, zoning out, anxiety, anger, and nervousness was out of control. I realized it was no longer safe for me or my family to keep my abusers' secrets. It affected the way I treated my family as well as my health which was worsening with unexplained symptoms. I would get dizzy spells, fainting spells and would zone out at work. I had memory loss and was having flashbacks and body memories. It was hard not to cry all the time. It was time to release my promises to my abusers and to break my silence.

Chapter 2
New Beginnings

While at work, I received a call from the police officer at Veronica's school. The sexual harassment allegations my daughter spoke to me about was only half of the story. The police, while investigating the allegations, discovered a group of underage children was playing the "Nervous" game, which consisted of fondling, oral sex, and ultimately intercourse with more than one partner girls on girls, boys on boys and boys on girls. I was shocked and silent as the officer asked, "Are you still there?" I responded, "Yes." She continued, "Both of your daughters are involved. This game was happening on the weekends with poor supervision on the part of your ex-husband." I had no response. The officer repeated, "Are you still there?" I responded softly, "Yes," as overwhelming disappointment, fear and tears started to emerge. She continued, "All the children are being charged with Sexual Assault of a Child since they are all under the age of 18 and because there was a fourth grader involved in the game." As I feel myself dissociating and slipping out of the present, I hear the officer tell me that I will be receiving the court papers in the mail and that I would have to be present at the hearing. She also suggested counseling for the children.

I was referred to *New Beginnings Counseling Center*. I called and told the receptionist, Susan, that my children were court ordered to receive therapy. I also informed her that I was a victim of trauma, had post-traumatic stress disorder and felt it was time to seek professional help.

She took my contact information and told me she would call me back after she consulted with the therapists about our situation. By the afternoon, Susan had counselors assigned and appointments were scheduled.

I was seen first because I had to explain why the girls needed counseling. As I walked into the lobby, I was afraid of the entire process. I wondered what was going to happen to my abusers once I told what they did to me. I timidly walked up to the receptionist area. Susan noticed me right away as she said, "Leslie?" I replied, "Yes." She had blond hair and was professionally dressed for her position. Her kind smile and gentle demeanor seemed to have a calming affect on me.

She handed me paperwork to fill out before the start of my session. When I reached the financial page, I was overwhelmed with the expense of care. Whatever my insurance didn't cover, I would have to pay right away at each visit. I understood why but I wasn't sure if I could afford it. I expressed my concerns to Susan and she told me not to worry. She would call my insurance company to ask questions about my coverage.

Then Susan introduced me to Sandy whom would be my therapist. I shook her hand as I noticed her long shiny black hair and her smile which showed her friendly aura. Sandy gave me a tour of the facility. She said, "I give a tour to all the new patients so they feel safe in the new environment." After the first room, I replied, "The rooms are pretty." The first room had elegant furniture with calming colors and a floral pattern on the sofa with soft fluffy pillows, beautiful artwork, fancy curtains, and the walls were painted with floral borders to match the theme. I also liked the massage therapist room. It had a massage table, soft music, a small table size waterfall with water softly trickling down the rocks. The atmosphere in the room felt relaxing, safe, and healing. After the short tour, we went to her office.

I feel my heart beating fast and panic sets in as we walked down the long hallway. As I entered her office, it seemed very cheerful with two purple sofas and fluffy pillows, with some artwork on the wall. She had a desk in the corner and two windows. She retrieved my paperwork from Susan and began our session. She asked, "Leslie, can you tell me why you and your daughters are here?" I cleared my throat as I admitted with shame that my parenting wasn't enough to keep them out of trouble. I explained, "They are court ordered to be in therapy because of the sexual game they were doing with friends while at their dad's house on the weekends. Also, they were molested by three of their step-brothers when they were six and eight years old." I reported, "I had an investigation opened but there was no evidence that anything happened. However, Veronica talked about it again while being questioned by the police of why the nervous game occurred."

"For myself, I have experienced a lot of trauma and neglect that I feel I need help with." She replied, "I see." "I think I have enough information about the girls but let's use the time left to talk about you." Inside I was panicky but Sandy had a kind face and I felt I could trust her. I began with the abuse that occurred. "I am not sure if you will believe me because I have had many abusers in my life." She replied with a reassuring voice, "When children grow up with abuse, they are not taught the tools to find non-abusive relationships because of the lack of boundaries which leads them into more abusive situations."

I decided to start my long list. It felt like I was talking about a grocery list. I had no feelings or images associated with it, just that it was a list of abuse and neglect.

I explained, "I have no details, just an overview of my life." "I don't even remember my childhood, only that I suffered many injuries and never felt loved or safe." Sandy reassured me, "It is normal not to remember much. Your brain repressed your memories as a coping mechanism." Sandy replied, "That's a lot to go through." "How do you cope with all of this?" I told her my previous counselor informed me that I have PTSD (post-traumatic stress disorder) but never really explained it to me. I spoke about my panic attacks, dizzy spells, flashbacks, nightmares, and my angry outbursts with family. Lately, smells and loud noises upset me and the repeating of words, etc. I said, "I try to take hot baths to relax but with three children, I never have uninterrupted time by myself. I am always nervous, in fight or flight mode and crabby all the time."

She explained, "These are all symptoms of your PTSD." I asked, "Does that mean I am going crazy?" She replied, "No, but until you deal with all of your trauma and abuse they will remain and will even get worse." I then explained that I have been having strange health issues too and the doctors can't find anything wrong with me." "I fainted at the movie theater and woke up in the bathroom with hives and welts all over my body while people were staring at me, asking what happened." "I was at Subway and experienced all the symptoms of a stroke: memory loss, couldn't speak, read or communicate, face and body went numb." "Both times 911 were called." She said, "It is all connected." "Our time is almost up but let's schedule more appointments. "I want to see you every week if not more but we will try weekly first." I told her, "A lot of weight was lifted off my shoulders and that I felt better." She seemed happy for me as we walked back to the reception area. I watched as she instructed Susan about my care plan. Then Sandy said with a smile, "I'll see you next time."

I was still worried about my insurance so I asked Susan. She said, "I have good news. Your insurance is a good one and not to worry because the first six sessions are free. Then you have a deductible of $1,200 and then you only have to pay $18 dollars a session." I was relieved because I had $3,000 in my Pay Flex account.

Chapter 3
Tears Start to Fall

I sat in the lobby and waited for my name to be called. I was nervous as I caught myself biting my nails to the skin. I was obsessing about what I would talk to Sandy about today. My mind felt blank. The longer I sat the more nervous I became as my eyes started scanning the room. I gazed up at the ceiling and noticed something hanging. It was a cluster of different circles on different levels, in a variety of colors and was moving slightly. My eyes were fixed on it and I noticed myself calming down.

Sandy called my name with a welcoming smile. I noticed she had on a pretty black shawl that covered her arms. Before I reached the doorway, she asked, "How is your day going?" as she observed my answer. I responded, "It has been okay but I am nervous about what we will discuss today." She told me not to worry.

We walked down the long hallway to her office and I took a seat on the sofa. Sandy could feel my anxiety. She leaned forward in her rolling chair and said, "We'll go step by step, okay." She had compassionate eyes and I felt that my comfort level was very important to her. She opened my file and gently explained my care plan and treatments that she would suggest for me. She explained the, *EMDR (*Eye Movement Desensitization and Reprocessing) and Brainspotting methods and told me that in combination they will work well for my post-traumatic stress disorder (PTSD). She explained, "The brain spot is where your memories are stuck and frozen because they were not processed correctly during the trauma. This is the source of what is causing your PTSD symptoms. Your brain thinks that what is happening to you while you are triggered is in the present. Your brain doesn't recognize the trauma, abuse, and parental neglect are in the past. With the EMDR and Brainspotting methods, we are trying to reprocess those memories. Then your brain will recognize you are no longer in danger and that it happened in the past."

After she explained the process, she asked, "Do you have any questions? Do you feel comfortable trying it today?"

I said, "Yes, anything that will reduce my PTSD symptoms would be helpful."

Sandy said, "Don't worry if it takes a while for memories to come back. It could take a week, a day or a year before we get anything but we will keep working on it."

She started by asking me to put headsets on. I heard two tones and soft music playing in the background. She explained, "With EMDR the two tones help to stimulate memories in your brain." Then we found what was called the brain spot. She took a pointer and had my eyes follow the tip until we found the spot that held the highest place of anxiety. She said, "The brain spot is where the memory is frozen in time."

She told me to keep my eyes on that spot behind the pointer which was the corner of the picture frame. She instructed me to concentrate on that spot as she took the pointer down.

Then she asked, "What do you want to discuss today?" I told her, "I am not sure." She said, "Take your time and let me know what comes up as you sit there for a moment." I replied, "I don't remember my childhood." "All I remember is feeling unloved, unsafe, and the only time I felt loved was when I was injured and my parents were literally trying to save my life." I explained, "All I remember is several injuries as I named them all off and the house fire." I felt the little girl panicking inside as an overwhelming feeling of shame surfaced as she explained what happened while fidgeting with her fingers and bouncing her leg nervously:

I am three years old. My sister, Victoria, and I love the smell of matches. She tells me to get mom's attention while she takes the matches. I go downstairs and ask my mom for a peanut butter and jelly sandwich. While my mom makes the sandwich, my sister takes her matches from the table where she left them. I snuck out of the kitchen with my sandwich and join Victoria upstairs. I want to light the match but my sister said, "No, you're too little!" She lit the match as she is standing on the bed. When the match gets too close to her fingers she drops it. Then she continues to light the second and third match. Before I knew it the bed was on fire. I panic and try to put it out by throwing my toy piano on it. It got bigger. Then I threw my stuffed animals in the fire and it got even bigger. My sister just stands there in shock as I try to put it out. I escape to get help when the curtains catch on fire.

I was too little to walk down the stairs, so I sit down and quickly bump down the stairs on my butt. I run to my mother and scream, "Fire momma help!" My mom laughs because she thinks I am joking. I plead with her to come upstairs and check as I push her toward the stairs. She slowly walks up the stairs as I urge her to hurry. To her terror, the entire room was on fire with my sister stuck in the middle of the room. My mom grabs my sister and runs down the stairs while yelling at me to go faster as I bump down on my butt.

We live in a small town with volunteer firemen. My sister and I are put safely in my grandma's, Angelica, car as we watch the house burn. From a distance we see our uncle, Nead, of whom we are always afraid. Then we panic as we think he sees us. We quickly hide in the backseat of the car. We feel really guilty and are afraid of what is going to happen to us. After the fire was put out, my uncle comes to the car and opens the door with his scary demeanor. He said "I want to show you something!" as he walks us back into the house and up the stairs. When we reach the top, he screams, "Look at what you did!" As we look around, there are only the blackened burnt frames where the walls used to be and it took up the entire upstairs. We cry at the sight of what we did and witness the smoke still smoldering.

I am feeling deeply panicky inside, at fault, unloved and naughty. No one cares that we are okay just that we destroyed the house and the fact my parents are renting. My uncle asks, "Are you going to play with matches anymore?" We both shake our heads, not saying a word, showing we will never touch them again. The little girl felt naughty when she said, "That is all I remember. I'm sorry," with tears rolling down her face while fidgeting with her fingers, as Sandy reached for a tissue.

She gently reassured the "child within", "That is okay because as we have more sessions you will remember more. We will stop here today and pick up again next time." She instructed me to take off the headset and release my brain spot by breaking concentration on the picture frame. I became present in the room again as the adult. She said, "Take good care of you, because we opened the gateway to the memories by doing the EMDR and the brainspotting. You may remember more memories by your next appointment."

My memories were repressed for 32 years until my first session. Then the flooding occurred and the memories came out so rapidly that it put me in crisis mode: I was with my family at a church fish fry. All of a sudden I felt an overwhelming feeling of being unloved, unsafe, unprotected and scared. I scanned the room and everyone was laughing and having a good time with their family. I was overwhelmed at the sight of people's faces and their voices were too loud which seemed to fade in and out. One minute I am laughing with my children and the next minute I felt an overpowering need to escape. I abruptly told my husband, Ramone, "We have to go!" I exited out the side door of the church, without an explanation. When my husband reached the van with our three children, I was crying hysterically. The children asked, "What happened mom?" I was unable to answer them. My husband carefully entered the driver's seat and softly asked, "What is wrong?" With my eyes overflowing with tears, I told him, "The memories are starting to come back but also the feelings of the vulnerable child are also coming back." The more I remembered the more unstable I became and couldn't wait to see Sandy.

Flashbacks in Post-Traumatic Stress Disorder: Surviving the Flood

I needed to release all the new memories but my next appointment was three days away.

I isolated myself from my husband and children. I lost complete control of my emotions. There were too many flashbacks of my childhood flooding my mind and it overpowered me. My adult self was broken as I witnessed what the "child within" saw and experienced as the accidents occurred. I did what Sandy told me. I took care of myself by taking candle light baths and got plenty of rest. I had to somehow regain control of myself because I had to work the next three days. My husband and children were concerned. I told them I had to release the old memories and reassured them I would be fine. I explained the therapy I was doing would help me heal from all the hurt inside. My family took turns checking on me to make sure I was okay.

My daughters, Veronica and Sabrina, came in and sat next to my bedside. They dried my tears and said, "Mom let's try to think of happy thoughts from your childhood." I tried to stop crying and straighten up for them. I said, "Let's see my grandma, Angelica, was where I have a lot of good memories." The little girl emerged as she pops up to a sitting position as she started to reminisce about her loving grandmother:

I remember going to the annual firemen's picnic. We have plenty of food, games, music and excitement. My favorite part is the huge pile of sand. My daughters asked, "Why was that your favorite part?" I explain, *"There is money inside for the children to dig out using only their hands.* My daughters agreed that would be their favorite as well. Then another memory enters my mind.

Before walking to my grandmother's house to her birthday party, we are greeted with a bat in our house. We watch as my dad takes a broom trying to catch it. When he finally did, we start walking to grandma's house. I want to carry grandma's cake. My mom said, "No, she'll drop it!" and my dad argues, "Let her." He hands me the sheet cake as I struggle to keep balance with my tiny arms, as they teeter tauter. The sidewalk ahead of us was missing a section and was replaced with sand. There was a little dip and I was waiting for it but I trip and the cake went airborne and lands in the sand. I begin to cry, "Oh no grandma's cake!" My dad scraps it off the ground, as my mom was angry because she told him not to allow me to carry it. I whimper the whole way there. When we enter grandma's kitchen, I run to her crying as I bury my head in her apron. She asks, "What is wrong?" My sisters tell her, "Tweetie" dropped the cake and mom yelled at her." My dad gives the cake to grandma as I tell her, "I am sorry for dropping it." She tells me, "We don't cry over spilled milk so we won't cry over a little sand in the cake." I watch as my grandma fixes the cake by scrapping off the frosting. We put the candles in it and sing happy birthday. My mom was the only one who didn't have any cake. My grandma said, "It is her loss because this is the best cake I ever had, all the more for me," with a great big smile.

The happy memories seem to be coming faster as I am glowing with happiness as I tell more memories:

My grandmother cooks with each child individually. She asks each of us what we want to cook. We then get our shopping lists together and we all go to the grocery store for our supplies. I always cook the same thing rice crispy treats. One thing you can count on with my grandma is if she is carrying a huge coffee can that isn't what is inside. It was always brownies, cookies, rice crispy treats or fudge.

After dinner, my grandmother would offer everyone tea and we are no exception. I feel special as she asks, "How many lumps of sugar and cream would you like?" We take our baths, get into our pj's and sit at the dining room table as grandma gets our bedtime snack ready, which was usually milk, a block of cheese cut fresh along with Ritz crackers. We pull out the bed in the couch, lie down with grandma snuggling us as we fall asleep to the Johnny Carson show.

When we had colds grandma would rub Vicks on our chests and put some under our nose.

Flashbacks in Post-Traumatic Stress Disorder: Surviving the Flood

My grandma has a way of making each child feel special. She bought each child a beautiful stem glass. Each glass is unique because each glass is different. She picks certain times when we will use them so they remain special.

My daughters' ask to hear more good memories of their great grandmother, who they never met. I respond, "Let's see" and as I start to flashbacks to a more loving and safer time, the "child within" told more of her memories while she sits on her knees rocking back and forth:

I always went with my grandmother to the grocery store. If I am good she gives me a quarter for the bok bok machine. It is a bird that sits on her eggs and when the quarter is inserted it would say "bok bok", as the egg drops into the hole. I am excited as I retrieve the egg and quickly open it to see what is inside. We live in a small town so the lady is always nice to me and calls me Tweetie, my childhood nickname.

I felt the adult surface as I told the children. "When I was going to Michigan at the age of 27, I stopped at the grocery store and I was getting a few things." I heard from behind the counter. "Is that you Tweetie?" I was surprised the lady, now elderly, was still there. She opened the cash register as she handed me two quarters for old-time sake. I had to hold back the tears as I felt my grandmother, Angelica, was reaching out to say hi. We reminisced about my grandmother for a while and I thanked her and gave her a hug.

A flashback to a sad time surfaced as I asked the girls to please let me sleep. I am tired. They both gave me a hug and thanked me for the stories about their great grandmother. I held the tears back until they left the room as the "child within" surfaced along with the feeling of loss; the tears began to run down my face dripping on to my pillow:

I am in sixth grade and so happy because I am in a play. I am singing a duet with my friend, Stella. We sing "The sunshine man." I went out for ice cream with my friend and her mom, Anne, before I return home.

As my happy face enters the house, it quickly turns into concern. My father is kneeling on the living room floor hugging my sisters and mom all are crying. My dad looks at me and says, "Come here Tweetie. Your grandmother died."

I didn't believe it. She wasn't sick. I am in shock when my father tells me that my grandmother had cancer. My family kept it from me because they thought I was too little to understand. I am angry because I didn't get to say good-bye. The last visit I wasn't allowed to go but my sisters did. Now I know why.

A flashback surfaced of my last visit with my grandmother:

I had a feeling something was wrong with my grandmother but thought she was lonely for my grandpa. Earlier that year, my grandmother and I went on our special walk with the dogs as we done many times before. She was quiet. Her face had worry on it as if she was searching for the right words to say to me:

She looks at me and says, "Tweetie, I realize you are older now but do you remember what you told me about your grandpa when you were five?" I reply, "Of course I do." "I said that grandpa was up in the moon and when you are lonely for him all you need to do is look up." "When it is a banana shape moon he is sitting and looking down on you." "When the moon is full, he is standing up waving to you." She looks at me with delight.

"You don't know this but that brought me so much comfort. I know you are old enough to realize that your grandpa is not in the moon. However, I want you to remember me and grandpa together in the moon when I pass away someday." I reply, "That will be a long time right grandma?" She smiles without answering.

As an adult now, I know she was trying to warn me that she was dying but I didn't have a clue so when it happened I took it really hard.

Flashbacks in Post-Traumatic Stress Disorder: Surviving the Flood

I don't remember a funeral for my grandmother but some time passed and my father wanted to go visit my uncle. Shortly after we arrived, he asked my dad to examine a package he received a while back. He wasn't sure what it was. My great uncle, Charlie, was almost blind.

My dad opens the package. He is in shock to see it was his mother's ashes. He said, "I thought my mother was buried!" He hands me the black box and we walk to our small town cemetery. Next to my grandpa's plot are boards covering a hole which was supposed to be where my grandmother was buried. Her gravestone is in place so my dad removes the boards and tells me to put the black box in the hole.

I try to be brave but tears begin dripping down my cheeks, as I had to say my good-byes to my grandmother again. When we finish burying her, we walk back in silence, while I am in disbelief of what just happened.

I had to make myself think of happy memories to find strength inside to be able to go to work in the morning. The playful three year old child remembers summer-time fun with Victoria as her tears dry and is replaced with joy:

My sister, Victoria, and I go to the baseball diamond across the street from our house. We play a game we call salt and pepper. The salt is a big mountain of dry sand and the pepper is the wet sand deep down in the ground. We gather the salt in piles then the wet sand is put on top and is patted down firmly. We repeat this process around the entire area. The holes always miraculously disappear and the next time we go we start all over again.

We live about a half-mile down the road from our favorite swimming area. My sister and I walk in the summer heat to go swimming. I remember getting too close to the strong current and being carried downstream while screaming for my sister to save me. Thank God she did each time. We also know to be careful not to go too far out because there are sudden drop offs from where the sand would shift.

In front of our house, the road was worn down making a large dip so when it rains it fills up with water. We are happy because we run in the house to get our swimming suits on. Then return outside to swim in the puddle on the side of the road. We laugh every time we see the lights in the sky.

My mind reached a point of exhaustion as I go to sleep. I awoke in the morning and as I get out of bed I fall to the floor because my legs felt weak. I wasn't sure what was wrong but it was like the time I had the symptoms of a stroke and the doctor found nothing wrong with me. I ignored it and sprung to my feet and wobbled to the bathroom to get ready for work.

Chapter 4
Family History

The day finally came and I was anxious to tell Sandy what I remembered. We got ready as we did before with setting up the EMDR and finding the brain spot. I started by telling her, "My parents, Paul and Rita, had a lot of their own problems and shouldn't have had four children."

"My mother was an alcoholic, for part of my childhood, and grew up in an abusive alcoholic home. My grandmother, Maggie, had a seizure disorder so my mom was expected to fill in as the wife. She cooked, cleaned, and took care of my grandmother when she had seizure episodes. My grandfather abused my mother her entire life until she moved out at the age of 17, when she married my father. In order to keep the peace between my grandfather and my grandmother, my mother had to dance with him all night until he passed out. Her brother left home at sixteen because he couldn't stand being beaten by my grandfather when he tried to stop him from abusing his sister and his mom. When my mother and my uncle, Dan, became adults they both used alcohol as their coping mechanism."

"My father had two jobs to support us. He worked as a painter and also he had a band that played in the bars on the weekends. My mother was so jealous of the women who would flirt with him that she had to be with him wherever he was playing each weekend. She started to drink socially but then it became she couldn't live without it which developed into alcoholism."

I was younger than five years old when my mom brought my sisters, Victoria, Sonya, and me to the bar. I started to feel the "child within" surfacing and the feeling of terror, being unsafe, unprotected, having no control, and my stomach started to hurt as I took a soft pillow for comfort:

I remember the bar being connected to the restaurant. I feel hesitant to walk in as I pause in the doorway while feeling frightened and alarmed. I see a pool table, bar stools and the bar. It smells of heavy smoke and alcohol. My mother walks right to the bar and begins drinking as I watch grown men take my two sisters and start to dance, hug and kiss them. My sisters struggle to separate from the men as they laugh while mom keeps drinking and ignoring the situation. I feel panicky and don't know what to do so I just watch and witness my sisters' terror. Living in a small town this behavior seems normal and no one intervenes to help us.

"When I was two years old, I was told that my mother gave me a black eye and my grandma, Angelica, forced my mother into alcoholism treatment. My grandma threatened to call social services on her and the consequence would be that all of us would be taken away. My mother went into the treatment center and came home and didn't drink anymore but she was very nervous and crabby all the time. She would constantly yell at us because we would get on her nerves. Soda and cigarettes became her new addictions so she bought them before food, toilet paper or pads."

"My mother and I became best friends when I turned eighteen, found myself pregnant as a junior in high school and was married to an abusive husband. She wouldn't let me quit school. She was sober for 28 years and during this time she was my best friend and my biggest supporter. After my divorce, I thought my life was over but she proved to me it wasn't by staying up all night talking to me. My mom missed a lot of school days, had dyslexia, had poor eye sight and was unable to catch up when she tried to go to college. She helped me enroll in college by giving me the courage to try, even though I had low self-esteem. She took care of my children as I attended college so I wouldn't have the cost of daycare to hold me back. I received a one year degree as an Office Assistant, an Associate Degree

Flashbacks in Post-Traumatic Stress Disorder: Surviving the Flood

as an Administrative Assistant, specializing in software support, from a technical college. Then she cheered me on as I tackled a Bachelor of Arts degrees in Business Administration and Marketing."

"Then she was brave for the both of us as she helped me to heal by reliving with me her pain as a neglectful parent and with her own abuse memories. Then seeing her daughter suffer through the abuses she was unaware of due to her inadequate parenting skills. I love and forgive my parents because as an adult they are very supportive and loving to me and my children. Seven years ago my mother returned to being an alcoholic when she found out my dad was dying of cancer. Our visits are limited to her good days but I will never forget her support through one of the worst times of my life."

"My dad had post-traumatic stress disorder from the Vietnam War. When dad told me some severe stuff and because I felt unloved, his jokes weren't funny to me. They terrified me because I didn't know what to believe. The "child within" surfaced again while her lips quiver as she tells her story:"

I was two years old when my father was on a ladder and doing something on the roof in the dark. I am happily and safely playing on the floor with my toys when I heard a noise that startled me. I feel my heart drop as I became terrified. I look towards the window and hear a loud "Rouf" Rouf." I am so horrified I quickly jump to my feet dropping my toys as I run to the steps. When I am in front of the steps, I look behind me and feel the need to run but I was too little so I sit down, and bump down the stairs on my butt as fast as I can. I thought the doggy is running after me and was going to bite me. I reach the bottom of the steps and run to my mommy for protection. I catch my breath enough to tell her, "There is a doggy in my window," while I am shaking and burying my head in her chest for comfort and safety. As my mother is trying to make sense of what I am saying, my dad comes in the house laughing because he thinks it is a joke. My mom yells at him for scaring me. He tries to make amends but I no longer trust him.

Another incident occurred when I was three years old, my family and I had fun swimming in the river down the road from our house. On the way home, I remember sitting in the front seat beside my mom and dad while petting my new friend on my finger. I ask my daddy, "What is it?" He yells, "That is a bloodsucker!" I calmly ask, "What do bloodsuckers do?" He screams, "They suck your blood!" I become hysterical as I frantically begin shaking my hand trying to get the bloodsucker off my finger. It wouldn't fall off and I am in panic mode. I was afraid it would suck all my blood out. My mom tries to comfort me but it is no use because I am in such a panic it is hard to breathe. When we get home she pours salt on it and it falls off and restores me to safety.

When it came to discipline, my father would use a thick black leather paddle. He would get overly angry and disciplined us too harshly sometimes. My mother yelled at him that it was enough and would have to physically stop him from hitting us.

I remember being in the living room on a chair watching Sylvester and Tweetie cartoons when my dad brings my sister, Victoria, under his arm while she is kicking, screaming, and begging him not to spank her. After he retrieves the black leather paddle, he rushes her to the middle of the room and bends her over his knee and spanks her with the black leather paddle. After my dad stops she said, "It didn't hurt." My dad said, "Okay," and grabs her and spanks her many more times. I watch in horror as she keeps repeating, "It didn't hurt", as tears roll down her face and mine. I feel panic, terror, powerless and feeling unsafe as I witness my father's out of control anger. He keeps spanking her telling her to stop saying it and he will stop. I didn't understand why she provoked my dad that day but was thankful when my mom intervened again. After this episode, my mother finally took the paddle and got rid of it because his anger became unmanageable.

As the little girl is crying while fidgeting with the tissue in her hands, she feels the need to protect her dad as she tells of happy memories. My dad wasn't always angry, as a feeling of guilt surfaces for telling what happened. On payday, we would be waiting excitedly for him to come home. When we hear my dad opening the door, we all rush to the chair next to the door. As he enters the living room, all four of us leap on his back while welcoming him home with hugs and kisses.

He took us to McDonald's every payday and watch as we play on the playground going through the tunnels, down the slide, and tossing the plastic balls at each other.

He would give us each a dollar to spend at the candy store. My sisters would run ahead of me while I walk and enjoy the journey to the candy store, as I imagine what I will buy. I would arrive at the store reviewing carefully all the candies. There were tootsie rolls, gum, red hots, taffy, jaw breakers, tootsie pops and gum suckers. I would come home with a bag of candy and am so proud I bought it by myself.

When dad would play with us it was always so much fun because he would play the horsey game with us. All four of us would saddle up on his back. He is on all fours as he gallops around the house. When the horsey gets tired, he lies down as we bring bowls of water and food. Then the horsey regains strength to play some more.

There were good times but there were a lot of unsafe situations that became normal life to us such as my dad normalizing Uncle Tom's behavior of smoking pot and drinking large quantities of beer all the time. The entire family drank all the time so to us, children, that was acceptable behavior. The "child within" plays with her fingers nervously as she speaks about family secrets.

I am less than five years old. I recall a man approaching my father while yelling and threatening my dad in front of us because my uncle sold pot to his son. The man was so upset I thought he was going to hurt my daddy. He expects my dad to stop his brother but he couldn't control what his brother did. Uncle Tom ends up going to jail for a while because the police caught him growing pot in the woods but when he is released he continues.

I am so excited when my uncle and aunt invited me to a baseball game. My parents allow me to go with Uncle Tom and Aunt Violet to the game that was 30 minutes away from our small town. My Uncle Tom and Aunt Violet smoke pot and drink beer all the way there and back. I remember feeling like I couldn't breathe and am disoriented, trapped and sick because the windows are closed and smoke is filling the car. I try to stay low to the front seat along with my cousin who also came along to watch the game. I was so relieved when we reach home safely that I learn never to go in the car with my uncle or aunt again.

While my mother was still in the early stages of alcohol recovery, she notices my dad struggling with his post-traumatic stress disorder. It began with nightmares waking up in a sweat, angry episodes, feeling guilty for what he did in war to survive, which progressed into flashbacks to the Vietnam War while pulling knives out of the kitchen drawers in search for the enemy.

I remember one day I am about to walk into the kitchen my mom stops me with a panic look on her face as she keeps one eye on my dad as she tells me softly to stay still and not to move. I feel scared and frozen in place as I see the knife pointed at my mom. She turns her full attention to my dad who is holding a knife with a strange look on his face. Talking but I can't understand what he is saying. I witness my mom slowly and calmly walking up to him while repeating, "It is okay Paul I am your wife." "You are no longer in the war it is okay to let go of the knife." "You are home with me and the kids." She takes the knife out of his hands as he returns to the present and is confused as my mom hugs and kisses him saying, "It is okay honey. I love you." As they both cry while I am still standing there not understanding what happened.

Other times my mother would be panicking as my father is yelling for the enemy to come out of their hiding place. She would hide us in closets and throw jackets, shoes, blankets anything she could find so he wouldn't find us. She told us not to come out until she came for us. I was about 3 or 4 years old. If we have to go to the bathroom during the night, we urinate down the heating vent because we are afraid to go downstairs.

My mother attended a support group for wives with spouses that went to Vietnam War. The counselor told her to get us out of the house because she would be held accountable if anything happened to us. She tried to tell my grandmother, Angelica, that her son was mentally ill but she was called a liar. My mother had no place to go so she took us to a Caring House first and then she found an apartment. My mother ended up filing for a divorce but later my father received help and she took him back.

On June 22, 2005, my father was diagnosed with kidney cancer. He discovered this by accident when his appendix burst. The doctor broke the news to my family and me that my father had two months to live. He had a large tumor on his kidney which meant the tumor and kidney would be removed, small tumors on his lungs, spleen, pancreas, and small tumors on his other kidney.

May he rest in peace. He died on May 24, 2012.

During all of the chaos in our family life my sisters became out of control. The little girl again surfaces to tell the hurt she has inside while feeling unloved, not accepted, unsafe, and not part of the family. Her lips quiver, voice cracks as her leg bounced out of control. She tries to hold back the tears as she tells what happens with her sisters:

My sisters, Victoria, Sonya and Andie, and I had no parental guidance to know when the limits were reached and out of bounds.

My two older sisters, Sonya and Andie thought it was funny to throw me into a large pricker bush with berries on it in front of our house. They start at the front door and took me down the long porch. One would take my arms and the other my feet as I am kicking, screaming, and pleading in terror for them not to throw me in the pricker bush. Most of the time they swing me really high by the pricker bush just to scare me and to have control over me. Then they would put me down but I remember a few occasions where they actual let go and I fell into the pricker bush. As I am struggling to get out, my sisters are laughing trying to reassure me that they didn't mean to let go but I didn't believe them. I have scratches on my arms and legs. I was emotional scarred from this experience because I couldn't understand why my sisters want to hurt me.

I was the little sister that would tattle on my sisters so in retaliation they would put me in the closet upstairs. It had hooks all over the walls and it was a big walk-in closet. They knew I was terrified of the dark. My two older sister would overpower me and throw me in the closet as I scream and try to open the door they would be laughing. I finally give up sit down and close my eyes trying not to think of anything. I feel like our house was haunted because it was an old house and at night you would hear the house settling with many scary noises. I am terrified of the closet because I think I am going to die in there because the ghosts will kill me.

The only time I wasn't afraid of the closet was when my sisters and I set it up for Halloween. We put green slim on the door knobs and have fake spiders and cob webs. My dad plays scary music outside with his big speakers' underneath the porch. It was fun to watch friends go through our haunted house.

My older sister, Andie, always is the boss/parent so if I didn't listen to her then she would give me consequences. I remember she calls all the sisters into her bedroom for sister time. This time was very special to me because it meant we all climb in my oldest sister's bed and sleep with her, style hair, makeup and games. She was mad at me for something I did or didn't do. She made me sit in the hallway outside her room under the warm exposed light bulb on the wall while my other two sisters had sister time.

One of the fun sister times I remember is when my oldest sister let us help her with her Michael Jackson puzzle as we listen to her Thriller album. I remember trying to do the moon walk and dancing.

Flashbacks in Post-Traumatic Stress Disorder: Surviving the Flood

When my sisters wanted to be cruel again as consequences for me being the youngest and the big mouth of the family, my sisters would tell me that I am adopted and they are not my real sisters. I believe them because there are no pictures of me as a little baby. The only pictures I saw are of me four years and older.

In the summer we bore easily so one day my sisters, Victoria, Sonya, Andie, and I are playing at the school. My sister, Sonya, decides to use a coat hanger to pick the lock on the back door of the school. It opens and as we jump down off the ledge, we enter the gym. My sisters never did any damage they just enjoy playing basketball with a hint of danger. I sit on the sidelines as they play because I am too little to play, so they tell me.

One day they think they hear the janitor or something so they abandon me. I feel panic and desperation to escape as the heavy door slams shut. I am too little to leap up onto the ledge to free myself. Tears roll down my face because the dark terrifies me and all I see is the low dim exit light. I squat on the floor and wait, it seems like forever before my sisters come back to rescue me but when they finally did I was thankful.

I went with my sisters when they play on the railroad tracks. They put pennies on the tracks. When we hear the fast approaching train, we quickly dive into the ditch line as it passes with speed sometimes barely making it to safety. Later, we find out that my uncle, Rick's, twin brother was killed, at the age of five years old, doing the same thing we are doing!

I said to Sandy, "The saddest thing I remembered is that I didn't feel loved by my parents or my sisters when I was a fragile child. The only time I felt like they cared/ loved me was when I had accidents and they were trying to save my life." "Then all the attention was on me and I felt loved for a while."

Sandy asked, "What type of accidents are you talking about?" As the "child within" starts to feel scared and hurt, she sobs as she takes the pillow for comfort while hugging it. Sandy says gently, "Take your time and remember we can stop at anytime," I respond, "I have to get it all out because I cried all week at home and I need to heal." I told her all the accidents and trauma I went through and survived:

I am three years old. It is a nice sunny day and the grass is so green and I am walking to the school by myself to be with my sisters. A boy is approaching me and he is mad at one of my older sisters, Andie or Sonya. He asks, "Are you Andie and Sonya's little sister?" I respond, "Yes!" as he takes a big rock and smashes it over my head. I fall to the ground screaming as my sisters, Sonya and Andie, come running. My forehead grows as blood streams down my face. My sisters rush me home and my dad is very angry. He asks, "Who did this?" and my sisters tell him.

My dad takes me to the boy's house to show him and his parents what he did. Then we drive the 30 minutes away to the hospital. I am so sleepy and as I start to drift off, my mom yells, "Don't fall asleep!" "You many not wake up!" as she tells my dad to drive faster. I am happy because my mom is rubbing my hair with worry in her eyes. I can tell she loves me.

Another time, my sisters and I are playing hide and go seek. I run towards the grassy area where my sisters are hiding. As I hit the barbwire, I am flung backwards and I drop to the ground flat on my back. As I slowly sit up, I glance down at my four year old hands and realize blood is dripping from my face and mouth. I look upward to see the thin piece of barbwire and I panic. I spring to my feet running towards the house with my arms swinging as if to give me momentum to run faster while I am screaming, "Help me!"

My sisters think I saw something that terrified me. As they laugh and come out of their hiding spots, they start the journey back to the house to check on me.

I reach the porch with trembling and bloody hands. I open the door. I am standing in the doorway and see my mother sitting on the sofa visiting with her friend. I screamed, "Mommy help me!", as I hold up my bloody hands. She screams, "Oh my God, what happened to you?" as she looks closer at my face with a portion

Flashbacks in Post-Traumatic Stress Disorder: Surviving the Flood

of my tongue hanging, almost severed. My mother panics as she rushes to get ice, a towel and to call my grandmother for help.

My sisters reach the doorway and have a look of horror on their face as they see me and start to scream and cry asking my mother if I was going to be alright.

My grandmother arrives at the house in minutes and we start the 30 minute drive to the hospital. On the long car ride, my mother keeps removing the towel and saying over and over again, "It's deep! Drive Faster!" My mother reminds me not to bite down and to keep my mouth open so I don't choke on the blood. I feel weak and close my eyes. My mom yells, "Don't fall asleep! You may not wake up!" I gaze into my mother's eyes and can see the concern and love she has for me.

When we reach the hospital, they rush me into the emergency room and have no time to freeze my face. There is a bright light over me as the doctors repair the open wounds. I watch their fingers in action as they quickly stitch my face. I try to be brave and not cry. I didn't want to give in to my emotions but my eyes begin to water and tears trickle down my cheeks. When I am all finished, the doctors give me stickers and on the way home we stop for chocolate malt at McDonalds.

When I am in first grade and my oldest sister, Andie, and I are at Aunt Betty and Uncle Nead's house alone. She is talking to a friend on the phone in the living room while sitting on a recliner. She orders me to get the fudge from the refrigerator and I return with it. She says, "This is too hard to cut." "Put it in the microwave to soften it up."

I go to the kitchen and I can barely see over the counter. I step on my tiptoes to put the fudge in the microwave and I press random buttons and wait. When the microwave beeps, I can't see inside the pan so I stick my middle finger up to my knuckle in the hot boiling fudge. I shriek with excruciating pain as I run around the house, while shaking my hand. My sister, Andie, drops the phone and tries to catch me to see what is wrong. The fudge was cooling as it stuck to my fingers. When she finally catches me and sees the fudge, she panics. My sister put my hand under cold water. She gently tries to remove the fudge from my fingers. My parents come through the door and all Andie could say is, "I am sorry, mom and dad, Tweetie got hurt." My mom gasps as she looks at my red knuckle but the alarming thing was my middle finger it's swollen and puss was forming in the finger.

My parents were really rough on Andie. I feel bad for her as she cries. The next day my parents take me to the doctor. He takes a needle and pops a hole on the side of my finger and then forcefully squeezes hard to release the greenish-yellow puss until the skin wrinkles and is hanging off my finger. Then he uses tweezers to remove the skin around the finger. He reassures my parents that the skin will grow back.

When I am in third grade, as I look out the window, I see the snow lying softly on the ground. I wish I can go outside to play with my sisters. We like to build snowmen, make snow angels, make forts and have snowball fights. We also go to garbage hill and go down it with our sleds. I can't do any of it this winter because I broke my toe and fractured my foot.

My second to oldest sister, Sonya, gives me piggy-back rides around our dining room table. When she goes around a few times, she expects me, the youngest of four girls, to give her a piggy-back ride. I try to keep my balance as she jumps on my back. She yells "gitty up" and leans backwards. I lose my balance and we both fall backwards with my leg bent backwards underneath us. I immediately feel pain as I shake and rub my foot crying for my parents.

Even though I was crying and in excruciating pain, my parents didn't take me to see a doctor. Instead it was simply time for bed. I kept crying and my older sister, Andie, got angry because she couldn't sleep so she threatens to hurt me if I didn't shut up. I muffle my sobbing under my blanket. I couldn't stop because the pain was so great. By morning, I couldn't bear weight on my foot so I hop on one foot as I tell my mom I couldn't go to school. My mom thinks I am trying to get out of going to school. Then my dad says, "I better take her in and get it checked out." I am relieved as we wait for the bus because I knew the doctor would know what to do to get the pain to go away.

Flashbacks in Post-Traumatic Stress Disorder: Surviving the Flood

The doctor confirms that I broke my big toe and fractured my left foot. He gives me crutches and wraps my foot. It was in the middle of winter and my parents didn't have a car so I have to walk to school on crutches. My arms are sore and raw underneath my under arms and I fall several times on the ice. I feel unloved because I couldn't understand why my parents didn't ask my uncle or aunt to drive me to school. My third grade art teacher would come to get me for class which is downstairs. Each day she gives me a horsey back ride to class and it was fun. I like the attention.

I am in fourth grade. My sisters and I are playing a game we call alligator. The game consists of two twin beds being across from each other and a person lying on their back on the floor. The person on the floor has their legs kicking in the air. The object of the game is to jump from side to side without the alligator touching you. If the alligator touches you, then you become the alligator. My sister, Sonya, screeches, "It's your turn," as she pushes me from behind with force that causes me to fly across to the other bed, over shooting it with my hands both out in front of me. My left hand goes through the window as my right hand hits the wall

My sisters all scream, "Are you ok?" As I look at my wrist with glass and blood squirting upward, and a hole in my wrist I knew it wasn't okay. I panic as I quickly run downstairs to go find my mom. My dad in a panic runs in the winter without a jacket to get help from my Uncle Nead who lives about five blocks away.

It was the longest wait for help because my mother is hysterical as she keeps trying to see how bad I was cut. "Did it cut your vein?" This gets me more scared as she repeats the question several times. I ask, "Mommy am I going to die?" I can see the blood squirting upward and a hole in my wrist every time my mom removes the towel. I am convinced that I am going to die and I wouldn't see my family again. My uncle, Nead, finally arrives and drives my dad and me to the hospital. I receive stitches and return home.

A couple of weeks later, my sister, Sonya, and I are playing the Vic 20, which was a computer with games. We have a chair that the cushion falls off and under-

neath is just the metal frame of the chair and the open floor. I always stand up when it is my turn. My sister thinks it is funny to take the seat off while forcing me to sit down. The chair has two metal pieces sticking out of it. As she takes the seat off and her hand forces me off balance, I fall. I feel pain immediately. When I get up, my pants are torn and my leg was bleeding badly.

I yell for my mom. She takes one look and says, "That is bad!" She quickly returns with a towel and peroxide. I scream as I run into the dining room and circle a table running away, begging my mom not to touch me with the peroxide. I know it would burn and the cut was too deep. My dad comes into the kitchen to check on the commotion. He looks at the blood going down my leg and agrees with me that it is too deep. He again goes for help to get me to the hospital.

The hospital workers remember me from the last visit as they interrogate my parents. I am asked over and over again "How did this happen?" "Did your parents do this to you?" I repeat my answer "No!" I keep repeating what happened and my sister's involvement. They continue to question me as I watch them put on the yellow soap to clean the area, the shot that froze my leg, and then the stitching of my leg. When they are all done, they finally believe me and allow me to go home.

Sandy looked at me in shock as she said, "You really have been through a lot and it sounds like you and your sisters weren't supervised. Wasn't there a social worker involved with your family at all?" I answered, "Not in a small town." She told me to take extra care of myself until our next visit as she reviewed the techniques to use if I needed them.

As I was about to leave Sandy asked, "Do you have an hour to do some attachment therapy?" I said, "Yes." She took me into a different room with a beautiful couch, desk, and table. It looked like a sitting room out of a magazine.

She gave me headsets and put on a CD as she explained this will help you get in touch with the "child within". "Listen to the woman's voice and imagine and repeat what she is saying. When you are finished you can give this to Susan and you are free to leave." Before she left the room, she took a blanket and tucked me in as a mother would do for her child before bed. I felt loved, secure, comfortable and safe. She dimmed the lights and left the room softly as the CD started.

A woman's soft calming voice started the session. She told me to get comfortable by breathing in and out and to imagine I am in a nursery and see a white bassinette. She tells me to walk towards it. As I do, I notice a newborn baby inside. She instructs me to carefully pick up the baby while guiding her head. She states that the baby is me. I notice a rocking chair across the room by a window. As I carefully walk towards it, I sit down and start rocking the baby while singing a lullaby to her. I feel calm safe while I tell the baby how much I love her and will care for her and that she is safe with me. I am starting to feel connected with myself as the CD continues.

The woman then tells me to imagine a safe place. I imagine my quiet place with a waterfall trickling softly onto the rocks, as I sit against a tree with green grass underneath me. Then the woman says to imagine that I have the baby in my arms and she is crying as she suggests that the baby is hungry. Then I imagine myself taking a baby bottle out of the diaper bag beside me. I start to feed the baby while remembering the baby is me and my adult self is caring for her. I start to cry because the baby feels loved, safe, taken care of, protected and innocent. I never felt this way but through the imagery I could feel what it was like to be nurtured. After the baby is fed, the woman asks me to tell the baby anything I would like her to know. I tell the baby that she is precious, beautiful, loved, safe, and that I won't let anyone hurt her. I will be her protector.

Then the woman tells me to repeat after her. "I deserve to feel safe." "I deserve to feel loved." "I deserve to have all my needs met." The session closes with more deep breathing as I return back to the room. I get up slowly and notice a feeling of calmness, a freeing feeling, and happiness as I leave the room to go home. As I reached the car, I realize my right eye is switching and the back of my head felt numb but I again ignored these strange symptoms that keep appearing.

Chapter 5
Pebbles Thrown into the Water

On a beautiful sunny day, I went into Sandy's office feeling sad but free because I knew that my grandmother was no longer a threat because she was dead. It still hurts me to think about what she did to me. As I explained it to Sandy, my "child within" surfaced to tell her story. The tears start to fall down my cheeks while fidgeting with my fingers and moving around unable to sit still as I shift from side to side.

My parents would take us to see our grandparents each weekend. My grandfather is an alcoholic so we wouldn't see them that much. We would drive the 30 minutes to see them but if he is drinking my parents put us back into the car and we return home. My mother told my grandmother, Angelica, to never leave us alone with her parents but supplied no explanation why.

When we are able to visit, we line up quietly standing behind my parents as they ring the door bell. As we walk single file into the front door, grandma, Maggie, and grandpa, Fred, greets us with a warm hello. The children are led into the living room and told to sit on the couch. The adults stay a while and visit with us as we all sit quietly with our hands folded on our laps and spoke only when spoken to. I feel happy to see them but am fearful of them at the same time.

As we sit there, I look around the room in awe of all of grandma's pretty knick knacks, pictures, colorful dollies, and knitted yellow, bright orange and brown afghans. I politely ask for a piece of candy from the fancy glass candy dish. Grandma says, "Sure honey." As I carefully take the top off, I accidently ding the top of it. My Mom quickly stares at her mother and father in a panic to see what their reaction is going to be. I apologize, "Sorry grandma the top is heavy." She responds with a kind smile and says, "That is okay." I sit relieved while looking down as I nervously suck on my peppermint candy.

When my grandfather has enough visiting with the children, he puts the TV on and that means all the adults are going to go into the kitchen to visit. Grandpa makes coffee and has coffee cake for them while they talk and play card games. The expectation is that all four of us girls stay on the couch and watch TV quietly. My grandparents are very strict. There is no room for playing or acting goofy, as they call it.

We were children ranging from 3 years to 9 years of age. We stay quiet for a while but we get bored. I either am playing with grandma's knick knacks or her electric chair. The chair is fun because you stand up with your butt touching the chair and as the switch is pressed it lowers down and you are in a sitting position. When we would get too loud, my mother would run into the living room acting nervous and begging us to calm down and to play quietly. I didn't understand why she was scared as she looks behind her to see if anyone is coming.

We are quiet for a while longer but then it is too much fun to play and jump around. We are especially excited when my cousin, Eddie, arrives because he makes us laugh, when we watch music videos on TV. When the "Who's Johnny" song comes on, he acts like a robot while the song is playing. Then quickly composes himself when my grandmother catches him acting goofy.

Some time passes and my other grandmother, Angelica, has us over for the weekends. This was during the time my parent are separated and stopped visiting my grandparents. Grandmother, Angelica, thought she is being nice sharing her time with my other grandma, Maggie, and grandpa, Fred. After a while my grandmother, Maggie, asks if we can sleep over on Saturdays. My grandmother, Angelica, allows it seeing no harm.

We are so excited because my cousin, Eddie, would also sleep over and we would have so much fun with constant reminders to be quiet or go outside. My *grandfather would be drunk. We see him scream at my grandmother and she tries to cover it up as she dry her tears.*

There are times I witnessed grandpa pushing grandma really hard as she falls to the ground and as she is lying on the floor he threatens to hit her. I run to her to help her up and she tells me, "Grandpa didn't mean to push me so hard." He would also tell her the house wasn't clean enough as I witness her repeatedly vacuuming the kitchen until he is satisfied.

All of us kids would escape outside to play and wait until dark to go back into the house. By that time, my grandfather is asleep… We then continue our fun by watching music videos and Creature Feature. We also take turns going into the kitchen to get everyone a cookie from the cookie jar. It is a scary task and only the brave ones do it because we didn't know what would happen if we are caught.

I dread the morning because that meant breakfast was coming. I was only three years old. Entering the kitchen, made my body feel like vomiting. I remember praying to God each day that I would be able to eat all the food that my grandmother, Maggie, put on my plate. It would consist of three hard boiled eggs, two pieces of toast, and bacon or scramble eggs with two pieces of toast and bacon along with a glass of skim milk, which taste spoiled to me. When I couldn't eat all the food, I was forced to eat it until it was gone.

I remember my grandmother telling me, "Your grandfather works hard to feed this family and you are not going to waste any food!" I would reply, "Grandma I am so full." "I can't eat anymore." I beg, "Please don't make me eat anymore." She threatens me, "If you don't eat that food by yourself, then I will make you eat it." I try to eat it like a good girl and often times get sick afterwards.

There are many times I couldn't eat it and she responded with forcing me to eat it. She would shove the food in my mouth then she place her hands over my Mouth and yells, "Swallow it!" as she holds my mouth closed and squeezes my nose so I can't breathe.

My sisters try and come to my aid by screaming, kicking and jumping on her back until she let me go. I am then able to try to swallow it but many times my sisters couldn't help me. I choke on the food and am panicking as I gasp for air. If I spit it out, she forces me to eat it again until my plate is clean.

Afterward she would tell me, "I knew you could eat it all, now go play outside." I would go outside and cry and wait for my grandmother, Angelica, to pick me up.

I would be so glad to see her but wouldn't tell her what happened. I wondered why my grandmother, Maggie, is so mean while my grandmother, Angelica, is kind and gentle. At her house When I am full that is okay. She takes the uneaten food and makes slop buckets for the dogs to eat it.

I am not sure how many weekends we slept over before my grandmother, Maggie, was caught abusing me by my grandmother, Angelica. When she got caught my grandmother, Angelica, screamed, "What are you doing?" as she took her hands off of me and told grandma, Maggie, "If I would have known you would abuse any of these children, I would have never agreed to have them sleep here!"

My grandmother, Maggie, explains, "We don't waste food in this house." My grandmother, Angelica, was so angry that she collects all of us children along with our belongings. We left and never slept there again. My grandmother, Angelica, was so angry at my mother for not telling her how her parents were because she never would have put us in that situation if she would have known that she would abuse me.

After my explanation was over, the little girl tells Sandy a happy memory about *grandmother*, Angelica while she excitedly bounces on the couch while tucking her feet under her body:

I am about 3 or 4 years old when my grandmother took us to the truck stop for supper. It is a secret of what we will eat. It ends up being banana splits. My sisters are struggling to finish theirs and I am going to prove to all of them that I can finish. My grandmother smiles as she says jokingly, "If you finish it, I will give you a quarter." That motivates me because a quarter is a lot of money as I daydream about walking to the candy store. I am almost done but struggling to finish the melted ice cream on the bottom.

I feel so sick it must have shown as my grandmother is begging me to stop while saying, "I will give you the quarter. Just stop!" But I wouldn't, a deal is a deal. Finally, I finish and I proudly collect my winnings. I barely get into the car without vomiting and the ride home was a challenge but I manage to get home. I have a bellyache the rest of the night.

After the session was over, I felt overjoyed to remember my grandmother, Angelica, a new sense of awareness and the need to heal became stronger with each session. Sandy continued to remind me to take care of myself and to communicate with my family when I needed time alone.

Chapter 6
Three Secrets

On a beautiful April day, I entered the lobby and was checking in with the receptionist. I broke down in tears rambling to her about what I remembered. She looks at the patients in the lobby as she quietly tried to calm me down with her gentle voice. She buzzes Sandy to let her know I was in crisis mode.

Sandy immediately appeared in the doorway as she called my name in a soft voice. As I walked towards her, she placed her hand out to receive me as I felt her hand lightly touching my back as she asked, "Honey what is going on?" She collected my files and her notebook as she sat on the rolling chair next to the sofa. Sandy didn't have to ask much. I was sobbing harshly with my chest moving up and down and barely able to catch my breath. I was talking too fast. Sandy slowly puts her pen and notebook down as she said, "Honey, take a deep breath in and out." We did it several times as I started to feel better and calmer. Abusive memories had been surfacing on its own. My friend's, Stella, brother tormented Stella and I. My memories included being sexually abused. I also witnessed Stella being abused by her father.

My "child within" defensively surfaces to explain, "I have no choice!" "When my parents didn't have food in the house, I have to go there so I can eat!" "This is how I survive!" I spoke about the guilt, shame and dirty feelings. "I participate in the sexual acts and no one makes me do it." Sandy asked, "How old are you?" I replied, "I am a second grader." Sandy listens as the "child within" tells her entire story. The child cries for herself as well as her friend. She expresses the guilt she feels for not saving her friend from her dad and brother.

I am in second grade when my family moves to Wisconsin. Our house is a block away from my elementary school. I remember the first day. I am skipping to school with so much excitement inside. I am eager to meet new friends and imagine how much fun we're going to have. From a distance, I see the school and as I get closer I am fearful but I continue. I arrive on the school grounds. I decide to play on the swings as I watch the other children play.

At first it is difficult to make new friends, my heart breaks with every insult and name-calling. They don't know me but have an opinion of me. I have brown hair, glasses, my eyes are crossed, and I have a scar on my face, and talk differently because the barbwire accident almost severed half of my tongue off. The children call me four eyes, say I am ugly while they cross their eyes to match what they see when they look at me. They mimic how I talk and tell me they hate me as they push me to the ground. I am sad, self-conscious and decide to avoid everyone by playing by myself. I try to convince myself that I don't need any friends.

It wasn't very long after I make that decision that a little girl approaches me. She has reddish hair with freckles on her face with a bright smile. She also had a few teeth missing. She says, "My name is Stella." "What is your name?" I reluctantly tell her and wait for the cruel joke to end but it doesn't end. She wants me to play with her and to be her friend. From that day forward we are inseparable.

I remember the first time I went to her house. I met her mom, Anne, and she is nice. They have many nice things. Stella excitingly shows me her room. It has big and high ceilings. She has so many toys I can't count them all. She asks me to play dolls with her, which is Stella's favorite. She shows me all her dolls. I am overwhelmed with excitement because she has a boy doll too, wow! I don't have one of those. I have one doll and two outfits at home. She disappears under her bed and pulls out a case where she stores her doll stuff. As I watch her tiny fingers unfasten the snaps on the side, I'm not prepared for all the wonderful things I will see. As she opens the case, it takes my breath away. She displays her dolls' dresses, pants, shirts, shoes, hats, and boots. Then she surprises me again when she yanks out a giant car. I hope this day doesn't end. I feel happy, joy, and lucky to have such a nice friend.

Flashbacks in Post-Traumatic Stress Disorder: Surviving the Flood

As we play, I hear someone coming. My attention reverts to the door and suddenly it flings open. The door makes a whoosh sound as the air hits the high ceilings with a loud bang. A young man comes in and rushes towards us and grabs Stella's doll and removes the clothes, head and legs as she cries and screams for her mom. I am so terrified. I just sit there and pray that I will be okay. Then from the living room we hear Stella's mom yelling at him to stop it, get out of there and let the girls play. He shoves Stella one last time. As he leaves, he stares at me. It gives me a chill and an uneasy feeling.

I refocus my attention on Stella and attempt to comfort her as she tries to dry her eyes. She says, "That is my brother, Frank, he always does that to me." We continue to play trying to forget what happened. I hear someone coming again! I begin to panic inside but as the door opens gently and her mother appears, I feel a sigh of relief as my body relaxes. She asks, "Would Leslie like to stay for lunch?" I stand up and accept her invitation with a strong, "Yes!"

I didn't want to admit how hungry I am because we have little or no food at my house most of the time. I am thankful for the free hot lunch we receive at school but on the weekends there is no school so there is no lunch. Stella leads me to the food pantry and says, "What would you like to eat?" As she asks this, she opens the cupboard doors. As I gaze up in amazement, because I never seen so much food in one place at the same time. I respond, "Where did you get all this food?" She replies, "My mom volunteers at the church and in return they give us food and she buys the rest." It takes me a long time to decide what we should eat. My eyes scan as my hands touch the boxes and cans. I finally pick the large beef vegetable soup. I glance at Stella with shame as I ask, "Can we have these crackers too," as I pull them out of the cupboard? She says, "Sure we can, soup isn't good without crackers," as she smiles. A sigh of relief comes over me because I didn't want her mad at me for asking for too much. I carry the soup in one arm and the crackers in the other to the kitchen. I approach Stella's mom and gently hand her the soup and crackers. She says, "Thanks Leslie."

She instructs us to go wash our hands as lunch will be done in a few minutes. I follow Stella back towards her room and to the left before her room are a few steps leading down to the bathroom. She hands me soap that smells so good and feels soft on my fingers. As I lather my hands with soap, we giggle at each other. I remember feeling envious of her because Stella has a mommy that loves and cares for her. My mom never tells me to wash my hands before I eat. As we dry our hands and go back upstairs, I feel my stomach growl so I walk quickly back to the kitchen.

The aroma of vegetable soup fills the kitchen. I notice as we stroll into the kitchen that there are four places set at the table. I sit in my place as her mother instructs, Stella sits in the other and her mother the other. There is one place left. My heart sinks as her mother calls Frank to come and join us.

As he enters the kitchen, I sense fear and try to avoid eye contact. His eyes stare at me and don't move. I concentrate on the steam that is enticing me to eat my soup. I reach for one cracker at a time. I put a spoonful of vegetables on each one while being careful to avoid burning the top of my mouth. Stella's mom asks, "Would you like a drink Leslie?" I respond, "Sure!" and expect to be offered water but instead she gives me choices of soda, milk, or juice. I excitedly blurt out, "Soda please!" I watch as she leans down next to the refrigerator and pulls out three-glass bottles of coca cola. She divides the bottles between the four glasses. She hands mine to me as I witness Frank glaring at me. Why doesn't he like me, I wonder?

We finish eating and I am happy to return to Stella's room to play some more. It starts to get dark and it is time for me to walk home. I say my good-byes to Stella and her mom as I slowly walk out the door. I bounce down the steps and am blessed because I am no longer hungry or sick from not eating. I feel like I am taken care of and at the moment have all my needs met. I walk with confidence all the way home. This is the best thing that has ever happened to me.

The next weekend, I return to play at Stella's house. As I enter her room, I notice how messy it is. Her mother demands that she cleans her room today. She stares at her room with an overwhelming look, as she asks for my help. She reassures me I'll receive a reward of a lunch and soda. I laugh and say, "I will help you without the reward because you are my friend." I secretly am thankful because I didn't have food at my house and am feeling weak from not eating. The night before, I had a piece of bread with mayo on it for supper. I had nothing to eat yet this morning and, if not for Stella, I wouldn't have lunch. I wasn't even sure if I would have supper tonight.

We clean her room, play and I notice the sun going down but I'm not ready to go home. I don't want to go to bed with another stomachache from not eating. It feels like the night never ends. I cannot sleep because all I can think about is eating. I hear someone coming and I sense no danger so I knew it was Stella's mom. Her presence is confirmed as she gently opens the door and asks, "Does Leslie want to stay for supper?" I jump up excitedly accepting her invitation. As I am eating, I see Stella's mom glancing up at me several times with compassion, as I ate quickly and ask quietly for seconds. Her mom responds by refilling my plate without me having to ask again. The questions in my head were: Did she know that I was starving at home? Did Stella tell? It didn't matter. I was just so happy to have the food in front of me. After we ate, I am respectful and help to clear the table as a way of showing my gratitude.

Then it is time to go home so I start walking. I am afraid of the dark so when I hear noises coming from the bushes it makes me afraid. I run the rest of the way home. As I reach my house safely, I slow down to catch my breath. I calmly walk up the steps to the long porch. When I reach my front door, I feel guilty for eating because I knew my sisters probably are still hungry. I go to bed but can't sleep wondering if my sisters had supper.

Days later, I return to Stella's house. She rushes me to her room to show me her new sleep-hide-away tent that she received from her dad, I think. It is a play tent that connects to a twin bed mattress. We are playing in her tent when I hear the familiar sound of Frank coming. Stella has a look of terror on her face as I reach to comfort her. I hear him barge in her room and the tent begins to shake violently as we hang on to each other for dear life. We scream for Stella's mother, she responds by yelling at him with authority to leave the girls alone. The tent stops shaking but we are paranoid that he is still out there. We wait for a while and I bravely unzip the door and look out and feel a sigh of relief that he is gone.

That night Stella asks her mother, if I can sleep over. She said, "Yes." I quickly call my mom to ask permission. My mom said, "Yes," so I go home to get my stuff. I am so excited! I couldn't wait to return with my clothes. This is one of many sleepovers we will have during our friendship. At every sleep over, three things are essential we need to have: Cool Ranch Doritos, Pepsi, and pizza. We stay up really late to watch: Car 54 Where Are You, Herbie, Nickelodeon, and the Andy Griffin Show. We challenge each other to see who can last the longest before falling asleep.

We continue to spend all our time together. One day, Stella calls my house and asks if she can come over to play. It is such a surprise that I go to meet her half way to walk with her. We run up the stairs to my room. Stella shuts the door behind us and locks it. I thought that is strange but dismiss it.

She says, "Do you want to play a game." I reply, "Okay, what do you want to play?" She responds, "I will show you the feel good game." I watch her demonstrate the game. She sits on the side of my bed, crosses her legs in front of her while bending at the knees, and lifts her body in the air with only her arms supporting her weight as she makes an up and down motion with her entire body. She says, "When you feel good you will know when to stop." She shows a few different ways of doing it but her favorite was what she demonstrated first.

After I see how much fun it seems and how happy it makes Stella, I try it. I decide to lie on the bed face down with a pillow bunched up underneath my private area. As I rock back and forth, I begin to feel warm. I keep repeating the back and forth motion until I reach a point where my body is throbbing and tingling. I didn't understand what is happening but I enjoy the way it makes me feel. I don't want the feeling to stop so I keep doing it until it begins not to feel good. I tell Stella and she explains that meant I did it too long and suggests next time to stop once I feel the throbbing. She reassures the feeling will stay around for a while after I stop moving. After we finish playing the game, Stella tells me not to tell anyone because we will get in trouble. She threatens that she will not be my friend anymore. I do not want to lose my friend so I promise not to tell. This is one of three secrets Stella and I will share.

As she leaves to go home, I feel naughty like I did something wrong but I ignore it because it makes me feel good. I continue this behavior whenever I feel sad so I can be happy for a while. Stella and I continue to play this game together at my house or hers. We both do what feels good separately and then would play other games as well.

As we are playing one day, her mother pokes her head in and says, "I need to go to the grocery store and then to check on your grandmother." "Frank will watch you while I am gone." As soon as she leaves, Frank barges in the room and says one word "downstairs!" Stella is in shock as she tells me to follow her. She looks different to me as she leads me, I ask, "What is downstairs?" There is no answer.

As I follow Stella downstairs to the basement, I feel sick to my stomach and fearful. It is cold, damp, and the room smells musty. Frank is already downstairs. He is lying on the table with his face covered with a cloth. I watch Stella's glazed eyes as she unbuckles his pants and something I never seen before pops out. It is pinkish-red flesh, large, and seems to spring out at us. As I watch with confusion and fear, Stella puts gloves on and begins to pull it while making an up and down motion. She speeds up and then slows down. She does this for a long time until liquid surfaces and I smell a strange odor. She takes a washcloth and cleans up the mess and throws it away. Then she takes the gloves off and discards them.

She returns back to normal as she states, "It's time for lunch," as she calmly grabs my hand and leads me upstairs. I glance behind me and see Frank getting up while smiling at me with his scary stare.

We enter the kitchen as Stella asks, "What do you want to eat as she opens the refrigerator?" She acts like nothing happened. She didn't have to tell me that this is the second secret I have to keep.

I lie to her as I say, "I am not hungry. It is time for me to go home." I walk slow not sure what to do. I feel naughty and sick even though I only watched without touching anything. I am numb and felt guilty and ashamed of what I experienced.

That day the food stamps arrive. Even though it was the feast part of the month, I couldn't enjoy the treats. At supper that night as I sit across from my mom and dad, I am paranoid that they knew I was bad. I feel my face heat up and am sick so I ate quickly and go to my room.

This occurs every time Stella's mother leaves us with Frank. For a long time it is ok that I didn't participate but then the rules change. Frank is on the couch instead of the table. His face is covered like before. Stella leads me to the sofa as I watch her unbuckle his pants while he lifts up his butt so she can pull them down further. I am terrified as she instructs me to touch it. "It's ok", she says. Then she tells me to lay on top of him with only my underwear on. I remember feeling something hard and warm on my private area. She tells me it is like what she taught me with the pillow. I did what I was told, as she watches me with Frank. I move up and down until the point of my body throbbing, tingling and my underwear is wet. As I am doing this, I pretend I am in my room and doing it by myself. When I am finished, I get dressed and Stella continues with Frank, as I watch. I feel ashamed and dirty and I hate myself.

Stella and I go back to her room and she tells me she wants to show me something. It was a book with naked people doing sexual things. She tells me that Frank does what is in the pictures to her when I am not there. She doesn't want to be alone with him when her mom is gone. I make the most impossible promise to always be with her so she wouldn't have to do what was in the book.

Some time passes. One morning my teacher announces to the class that we are going to the media center and will see a presentation. The presentation was about good and bad touches. I remember entering the media center and I rush to the front row and sit down with my legs crossed in front of me. I am wearing my favorite blue dress with white flowers with poufy sleeves. I am waiting excitedly to hear what she has to say. She first starts to explain that we will see a video then we will discuss it. As I watch the video, I begin to slouch and fidget with the corners of my dress. I thought I would get in trouble if anyone knew what was happening with Frank. As I see the examples of sexual abuse, I realize that what is happening is wrong and that I should tell.

As the movie finishes and the lights are turned back on, the speaker starts to move around the room. She looks down towards me and quickly I bow my head in shame to hide the tears that are streaming down my cheeks. I feel like the speaker understands what is happening to me. I want to tell her what is happening but feel trapped because I promised my friend I wouldn't tell. As I scan nervously around the room, Stella's eyes meet mine. I plead to break the silence, but Stella shakes her head and turns away from me with disapproval. I knew if I tell she wouldn't be my friend anymore. I need her to be my friend because she is my only true friend and I need her to continue to feed me.

More time passes. Stella and I decide to get our dresses on and to go play at the park. It was a sunny day with blue skies. We are so happy with little girl giggles as we talk on the tire platform, which are made of four tires that is shaped like a cube. We are on the top of the tires sitting across from each other. In the distance, I see a reddish-brown hair man shuffling across the street and up the sidewalk into the park grounds. I feel frightened and uneasy as he approaches us. I was about to whisper to Stella "Let's go home", when the man says, "Hi girls," in a strange creepy tone and then turns to Stella and says "Who is your friend?" I am in shock that she knows this man. Stella replies proudly, "This is my friend, daddy!"

Then Stella seems concerned as he creeps around the tire platform to my side. He says, "You look pretty today." as he takes two fingers and runs them from my ankle to my upper thigh touching the end of my skirt line flicking the ends with his fingers about to move up into my privates. At that moment, I remember what the speaker told us. I yell, "No!" with authority. Stella panics at my response. She quickly says, "Come on, daddy; let's go play on the monkey bars." As she pulls his arm away from me, and redirects him to play with her. He gives me a scary glance but listens.

Stella struggles to quickly climb the ladder, throwing her feet up to hook one of them on the bar, as she pulls herself the rest of the way. Meanwhile her dad is watching her dress flip up while her underwear shows. After she is settled on top of the monkey bars, his hands extend up over his head as his fingers disappear under her dress. As he does this, he repeats over and over again tickle, tickle, tickle, with his eyes staring at me. He is pleased to have a witness to his perversion.

I am exposed, not protected, frozen like ice, and feel at fault. As I watch Stella's dad abuse her, I think to myself, if I wouldn't have said anything maybe he would have left Stella alone. This was the third secret I shared with her.

When he finishes gratifying himself, he tells Stella he loves her with a passionate kiss on her lips. I watch him overjoyed as he walks out of the playground down the sidewalk across the street. He gets in his car and leaves. Stella calmly climbs back up on the tire platform, again acting as if nothing happened. It seems like a routine that she did over and over again.

I begin to cry as I tell her we have to tell. She looks down with disappointment and states, "Pat already tried to tell my mom and she didn't believe me." I decide it is time for me to go home. I am so confused why her daddy would do that to her. My daddy doesn't do that to me. I think to myself as I walk home, maybe Frank learned it from his dad.

Then the next time Stella's mother leaves it gets even worse. I am led to the basement like several times before. This time there is a bed near the couch. I remember sitting on the couch as Stella gets totally undressed. Frank is already downstairs with his face covered up. As I watch in horror, I see Stella standing over Frank. She instructs me to stand next to her and to watch what she is doing. She rubs her inner thigh with his penis. She says, "This is how you can trick him into thinking you put it in here as she points to her vagina." She wants me to try it but I wouldn't.

Flashbacks in Post-Traumatic Stress Disorder: Surviving the Flood

I return to the couch and look up and notice the basement windows have no curtains on them. I pray for someone to see us to stop it from happening. I would be hopeful every time I hear the neighbors come home. First, the car door open then shut but I just see their legs and hear voices fade as they go into their house.

This keeps happening for a few years until she tells me she has her period. I am old enough to know about periods and that she can get pregnant with what she is doing with her brother and dad. I yell, "You have to stop what you are doing with your dad and brother or you'll get pregnant!" She appears shocked, scared, and didn't know how to respond to me. We are quiet until she says, "It is time for you to go home." I am never asked to go to the basement again. I break my promise to her because she ends up being alone with Frank as her abuse continues and mine ends.

A while later Stella has surgery first on one hip then the other. She says, "The bones in my hip shifted over so I need to have surgery to put pins in my bone to fix it." I wonder sadly as I watch her struggle with crutches for each surgery whether it was because of what her dad and brother were doing to her small body.

We graduate from elementary school and enter middle school. Stella still visits her dad. One evening her mother was away at work. We are upstairs in her new house when we hear a knock at the door. Stella goes downstairs to answer it. I hear two voices so I go downstairs to see who it was. As I start down the stairs, I recognize the voice as being her dad. The closer I get I feel the familiar panic, and unprotected feelings as my heart begins beating fast and have the intuition to escape, like I experienced as a child on the playground.

As I enter the living room, I am sickened at the sight of them. They are on the couch with her dad's whole hand down her blouse fondling her breasts and kissing her as he displays a perverted look on his face. He is repeating in her ear "daddy loooooves yooooou." He reminds me of a sly snake slithering through the grass in search for his prey. She tries to separate from him when she sees me but he didn't stop. I show her anger and disappointment on my face because she lied to me. When I asked her if her dad was still hurting her she said, "No!" I told her it was time for me to go home. As I walk away, tears are falling because I couldn't get the image of her and her dad out of my head. Again, I feel guilty and ashamed that I didn't help her.

We begin to spend less time together but I was noticing a lot of changes in Stella's attitude. She acts very suspiciously because after each meal she goes to the bathroom immediately. I witness this over and over until one day I barge into the bathroom and catch her vomiting with her finger down her throat. I know from health class that she is bulimic. I scream, "I knew it!" "You are bulimic!" She denies it and didn't want to talk about it as she tries to justify her actions.

I am sick with worry because I know it is dangerous. I need to tell someone about it but who? I decide to tell her mother's friend. She knew it was me who told and this forever changes our friendship. She becomes distant and finds a new friend, Jessy. I still come over to see her but the closeness we once shared was gone.

The session again ended on a positive note as Sandy had me release the brain spot and turned the EMDR off. She used positive imagery to bring me completely back into the room as my adult self resurfaced and could separate the past from the present. Sandy continued to remind me to take care of myself as I left her office.

Chapter 7
Blinded by the Flood Light

Over the weekend, I slipped in and out of awareness. I had a headache that lasted four days. While I slept most of my weekend my husband, Ramone, took care of the children. I am far enough in therapy to know that I will have new flashbacks soon but do not know exactly when they will hit me. I shared with my husband that I needed to take care of myself.

On Monday, as I drove my daughter to school, I became numb and felt myself leaving the present to go to the past. From a distance, I heard my daughter, yelling, "Mom, are you taking me to school?" I jumped as I was startled and realize I was zoning out again. At this point, I was half way to my mother's house.

I turned the van around and got back on track as I apologized to my daughter, Veronica. She said, "Mom, I am scared that one of these days you are going to get us in an accident." We reached her school safely and I kissed her goodbye as I wished her to have a good day.

I then had to take my son, Kota, 4 years old, to his early childhood school. As we walked to the door, I started to sing a song I had forgotten. It was a song my deceased grandmother, Angelica, used to sing to me when I was little as I woke up from my nap. She would have a bright smile on her face to greet me. Tears began to stream down my face with happiness because finally I remembered something happy, as I sang, *"Wake up little chickadee, the sun is in the sky, the birds are eating worms and so must you and I. Wake up little chickadee."* Kota laughed as I sang and playfully swayed him back and forth. He said, "Again, again mommy!" As we reached the door, I set Kota down. I was about to go in the door but something caught my eye as I told Kota, "Come look at this with a soft voice" Kota said, "What mommy?" I replied, "See in the tree there are two bird nests inside." As I picked him back up with his face against mine, we both marveled at the beautiful tree with green buds.

Kota noticed little red buds on the ground. He said, "Mommy what's that?" I told him, "Those are red berries for the birds to eat." He glanced down at the ground and saw that the grass was worn and missing in the area under the tree. He said, "Oh, oh mommy." "Daddy needs to come to put grass right here", as he pointed with concern to the bare area. I laughed so hard because I missed these happy days because as of late I didn't see much happiness amongst all the trauma and flashbacks. We didn't see any birds but figured they must be asleep so we better be quiet, as we snuck inside the door. I waited anxiously for the teachers and friends to arrive to do our routine greetings in the morning.

I saw the teachers walking down the hallway. I felt really nervous because I wanted to talk to Kota's teacher. As his teacher greeted Kota good morning, I whispered, "Can I talk to you outside for a minute?" She appeared concerned but said, "Of course," as she excused herself reassuring the children she would return after she talks to Kota's mommy.

We stepped outside and I was choked up as I said, "I just wanted you to be aware that I have been through a lot of trauma and sexual abuse in my life. I have started to have flashbacks, body memories, and anxiety over it." I explained that my daughters were also going through similar issues due to abuse that occurred at their dad's house. She had tears in her eyes with compassion and concern as she put her hand out on my shoulder as she said, "It sounds like you have a lot going on. Thank you for feeling safe enough to tell me this. Kota is doing great in class. He is a model student and I don't want to give him up to the 4K program next year." She reassured me that she would let the other staff members know to keep a watch for any concerns and would contact me if anything surfaced. She

Flashbacks in Post-Traumatic Stress Disorder: Surviving the Flood

gave me a tight embrace and told me to take care of myself. We both returned to the group of kids. As I said good-bye to Kota, I felt glad that he was doing well and that I wasn't affecting his happiness because of all my crying and withdrawal from family time.

I returned to my van, got in, and slowly sat down. My heart was heavy as I began to cry hysterically. It was so hard to tell anyone about what happened. I kept it a secret for 32 years and now it seemed that is all I talked about.

I dried my eyes as I noticed I needed to be at work in 15 minutes. I sped to work, ran in the front door, quickly made my hot tea, and greeted the receptionist. I stared blankly at my computer screen. Suddenly my emotions overwhelmed me as I felt violated and trapped. The flashbacks began as I witnessed myself being raped at the age of 14 years old. I always knew that I was raped by my former boyfriend, Bret, but I didn't have the memories to be able to definitely call it rape. My brain repressed the memory until now. It started as small snapshots of the room arrangement, the door slamming and the rest of the memory quickly followed flashing fast from one frame to the next.

My hands supported my head as I weep and felt dizzy. Then I heard a calm voice say, "Hi Leslie are you okay?" as she carefully put her stuff down on the counter. I quickly sprung out of my chair and responded, "Yes!" I said, as I saw, Emma, my coworker, standing by my desk. With hesitation, she asked, "Are you sure?" I replied. "Yes, I am sure." I explained, "Just more memories." She stared at me with compassionate eyes as she said, "You are the strongest person I know and I mean it. You hang in there you'll make it," as she walked to her office and turned on the light. I quickly composed myself because my boss would be in soon.

A short while later, I greeted Emma good morning in her doorway with a famous Leslie's smile that reflected everything is fine, even when it wasn't. I needed to reassure Emma I was okay and told her not to worry about me. I felt guilty because I was concerned about affecting her happiness because she has allowed me to bend her ear and I didn't want to take advantage of it.

Then our boss arrived so I quickly got to my seat as we all started our day. We took photos of items for the facility rummage sale with a little side of silliness as our boss, Jenny, tried a robe on. It was what I needed to take my mind off of my flashbacks for a while. I was able to keep busy until about 4:00 p.m. when I realized I had to go to therapy soon.

I told my boss I had to leave 15 minutes early because I had an appointment at 5:00 p.m. She confirmed that she remembered and to have a good session. I was on my way to my therapy session and zoned out. I was half way there before I noticed. By the time I reached the door, my heart was pounding in anticipation for my counseling session. The receptionist asked, "Did you get my message that your appointment was changed to 6:00 p.m." I told her "No, I didn't get the message." She confirmed my cell phone number as my home number so we had to fix the number for future appointments.

I told Susan it was okay that I would wait in the lobby. I glanced out the window as I numbed out. I was not sure I wanted to tell Sandy about the most current flashbacks. I was frightened to speak about it in fear that somehow Bret would know and he would return to hurt my family or me. I heard Sandy yell, "I will be right there!" as she said good-bye to her clients.

Then her friendly face appeared and said, "How are you today?" I don't remember if I answered her as I passed her while she held the door open. On the way back to her office, she commented, "What a hectic day it has been." I sat on the couch as I told her, "It would only get worse with me." She replied, "That is okay. Sometimes that is how it goes."

Flashbacks in Post-Traumatic Stress Disorder: Surviving the Flood

She retrieved my file from her desk and sat down in the chair beside me with her notebook. I asked, "Do you remember what I told you about my former boyfriend, Bret?" My first session, I shared general information about each abusive relationship I had because that was all I recalled at that time." She replied, "So you are having more flashbacks?" I replied, "Yes!" as I felt the fear, anxiety, and heard the weeping echo in my head of a young girl 14 years old, begging me not to speak about what happened. I remembered what Bret said he would do to me if I told. She also reminded me of the haunting memory of what happened the first time I tried to tell, at the age of 15 years old.

I sit in silence on the couch as I feel the young girl emerging. I am hesitant to talk about what happened. My lips quiver and as I try to speak my voice cracks. I am on the verge of crying. Then I stop for a moment in a panic trying to catch my breath. I hear Sandy's gentle and comforting voice say, "Take some deep breaths in and out. Again take a deep breath in and out." I wasn't sure where to start. My memories were flashing so fast in my head that I am light-headed and sick to my stomach. Sandy could see my struggle as she offers me the fluffy purple pillows that are beside me. She directs me to hold the pillows in my lap while hugging them. She softly asks, "Is that better?" Strange enough, hugging the soft pillows gives me the courage I need to begin the session.

I admit, "I don't know where to start so I will start from the beginning." "I am 14 years old, in eighth grade. I am a slender, 130 lbs, good-looking girl that figures out very early that boys will notice me if I dress in tight shirts, jeans and short skirts. I need to feel loved and when I dress this way the boys give me the attention I am seeking. My parents didn't guide me one way or the other so I did what I thought was right for me."

I met Bret through Ben, one of my sister's older friends. I met him at a dance outside under the fairground's tent in the dark with colorful strobe lights. The crowd of people are laughing and dancing and the environment seems dangerous and out of control. I am excited because Bret is my first real boyfriend. I feel so mature for my age. I have butterflies in my stomach, my hands are sweaty and I'm nervous. As I look into his dreamy brown eyes with his long black hair, and charming smile, I feel truly and hopelessly in love. He wears tight jeans and is taller than me so I have to reach up a ways to dance with him. I feel a little adventurous because he is an older boy, junior in high school. I didn't have any parental guidance to stop me so I didn't know any better.

Bret is my entire life as he slowly separates me from my family and friends. Every day he demands to see me or he would get mad. He picks me up from school and takes me to his house to hang out, play video games, and watch movies. He builds fires in his parent's sitting room. We sit, talk, and kiss in front of the fireplace. He is romantic and kind. I am so in love with him and feel safe. I think he truly understands me, not like my neglectful parents who I feel didn't love or care for me.

We begin to take his car, ride around town and we always end up at Starlight Park in front of the lake. At first it was just hugging and kissing, while watching the lights across the lake and listening to the soft waves hitting the shore, with the smell of dead fish that I try to ignore. There also was other teenagers parking and running on the beach but we all clear out when the police make their rounds.

The more trips to the lake, the more advanced our relationship becomes. I recall feeling uneasy, as he touches my breasts under my bra and places his fingers in my pants while moving them around. The only contact I had with sexual behavior was the sexual abuse I experienced with my friend's brother, Frank. I want to keep him as a boyfriend so I did what he asks. I am dependant on his love.

The evening comes when it was my turn to touch his penis. I know what to do with my hands because while being abused with my friend, Stella, I witnessed her do it to her brother in the basement. I rubbed and jerked his penis in an up and down motion until he said, "Put your mouth on it." I don't want to do that, I never did it before, and panic set in. I didn't know what to do. No one spoke to me about peer pressure and that I could say no. He replied with a smile, "That's okay, I will tell you how," as he leans back in his chair to give me more room to be in-between him and the steering wheel.

I turn away from him facing the steering wheel as I put my mouth on his penis as he tells me "Draw your teeth back and suck on it hard." I scrape my teeth on it a few times, but then I am better. He tells me to go down more and more. As I try to be a good girlfriend, I go too far down and choke and almost vomit. He says, "You're a natural," as he put his hand on my head while pushing down firmly. Again, I almost vomit. I am trapped and want to stop but I didn't want him to break up with me so I continue, I gaze underneath the steering wheel at the dim dome light, waiting for it to end.

When he gets excited enough he ejaculates into my mouth, I open the car door while spitting the sperm out while fighting the urge to puke. I hear teens from the other car laughing at me. He receives high fives from the guy passing the car. I make the comment it tastes like pure salt, as he laughs. I tell him, "If I do that again, you have to warn me because that is too disgusting and that I don't want to vomit." He agrees and at future visits, he brings tissue to clean the mess.

One night Bret's parents are going out for dinner. We are watching movies in the living room. I am lying on the soft-carpet. Bret leaves the couch and lies next to me. He begins to kiss my neck, while putting his hand down my shirt gently touching my small breasts and putting his fingers down my pants. I wasn't alarmed until he removes my jeans and his jeans. I ask, "What are you doing?" He tells me he wants to have sex.

I said in a panic, "My mom will kill me if she finds out!" He promises, "No one will find out." As I sit up half way, I say, "I am too scared to go that far!" I explained that I heard that it really hurts the first time and there is blood.

He gently rubs my arm reassuring me that he will be gentle and I can trust him. Then I hear the words, "I love you." I needed someone to tell me that and so I give into him because I truly believe him. As he gets close enough to insert his penis,

I feel it touch my vagina when we hear the key in the door. We quickly put our jeans back on and act like we were watching TV the whole time his parents were gone. Shortly after, Bret takes his parents sports car and drives me home. I roll the window down to feel the breeze in my hair as I smell the fresh country air. When we reach my house, I'm a little afraid to go in, thinking my parents can tell I almost had sex.

 The next time we are alone at his parent's house, he did what he promised. Our first time having sex he was gentle and it only hurt a little. I feel guilty after we did it because I was terrified of my mother finding out because of the memories of my older sister, Andie. My mother shoves her and Andie shoved back with a little more force while my mother was screaming, "You are nothing but a slut and a whore." Andie tries to push my mother down the steps as my mom attempts to follow her to her room. My mom demands for my father to discipline Andie while yelling up the steps "You bitch, you're nothing but a fucking bitch." This fight was because she was 16 years old and my mother caught her having sex in her bedroom.

 I looked at Sandy and said, "I am not sure how much time had passed or how many times we had sex." As I took a deep breath, I continued to cry while feeling guilty and ashamed for having sex at such a young age, and fearful of what was going to happen to Bret after I told what happened. I began to tell her that I recall feeling violated like I was raped but that was all I remembered. I had no other memories until today, twenty-one years later. While driving my daughter to school, I zoned out and then at work, I had flashbacks throughout the day.

 The young girl's eyes flood with tears and can no longer see Sandy. I explain that he was talking to his parents down the hall in the kitchen. Then I hear the door close and his parents are gone. I hear Bret coming down the hall, as he appears in the doorway he says in an angry tone, "A girl accused my brother of rape. If that ever happens to me, I will kill her."

 At that moment, I am terrified of him because why would he tell me something like that. He slams the door with one hand behind him as he approaches me in a hurry. At this point, I am sitting up with my back against the wall. He begins to kiss me forcefully and it feels very different than before so I said, "No I don't want to." He replies, "Come on baby, you can't be a tease now", as he wraps his strong arm around my middle and pulls me down into a laying down position. I respond, "This doesn't feel right," as I try to get up. He forcefully takes his forearm and presses it against my throat to keep me from getting up. I am trapped, as it was hard to breathe. Tears of fear, disbelief and shock are pouring down my face. He lifts my shirt up while saying; "Give it a chance." as he begins to suck on my breasts. Then I feel extreme pain as his teeth scraps the tips of my nipples. My thoughts are racing inside my head. He is supposed to love me why is he doing this? All I can think about is the fact that I am not sure I know the way home if I try to get away. I know we are out in the country miles out of town. His arm releases my throat as he forcefully pulls my jeans off.

I don't remember him taking his pants off but I feel him trying to insert his penis but he has trouble because I am dry. He said in a creepy voice, "What's wrong baby, you are usually wet for me!" He inserts his fingers into my vagina without care and it hurts as he twists his fingers in different directions to try to open me up and make me wet.

I try to search my mind for a time when we kissed and had a lot of foreplay so I could get wet so it wouldn't hurt so much. He gets on top of me as he inserts his penis and his face is next to mine. I couldn't look at him as I attempt to lift his heavy body off of me with the palms of my hands but he pushes down harder with is body while saying, "You'll get into it. "You know you want me." There is no hope because I am in shock and fearful for my life. I turn my head towards the TV where we played video games and sat in the chair kissing and making out. In a fog, I remember being in love with him and needing to be with him every moment of the day.

I remember the romantic flowers he gave me and the fires in the fireplace when we talked about our future together. I loved the smell of his scent so I would wear his shirt home to sleep with it until we could see each other again.

I come out of the fog as I think it is over. I didn't feel trapped by his heavy body anymore. Then I feel something I have never experienced before. As I sit up half way and glance down toward the bottom of the bed, I see Bret staring at me with my pubic hair under his nose as he sucks really hard, clenching my hands on the side of the bed as I try to tolerate the pain. I remain lying down as I return my concentration to a numbing state of mind. I pray to God for his mercy and help for it to end. As I return to the room, Bret is standing by his dresser drawer and takes out a plastic container, shaped like a bubble with a plastic flat bottom. He turns to me while taking my public hair out of his mouth and says, "This is where I put all my bitches." It was that moment that I knew I wasn't the only one as I saw my hair added to the big ball of hair in the container. He looks as if his task is complete as he cheerfully asks if I am ready to go home.

I feel I don't have the right to call it rape because I didn't fight back. Why didn't I fight back? I was so angry with myself because even though he did that to me I didn't want to hurt him! I loved him and he was supposed to love me. I started to feel like it was my fault for the clothes I wore. If I wasn't so skinny or pretty then this wouldn't have happened.

Sandy said, "That is not true, it would have happened anyway. "It sounds like Bret had a lot of problems and was a deviant adolescent." Then she asked, "Did you go to the police?" I replied, "No, I was too scared because he said if I told anyone he will kill me."

I explained how upsetting it is to see the entire house in my head. I know where all the furniture was placed, all the exits and windows. His bed was a mattress on the floor, his closet at the foot of the bed with his dresser inside it. I placed my hands on my head while saying, "It is driving me nuts!" Sandy calmly explained, "It is because when you have trauma the brain freezes creating a snapshot that is stored in your brain until you can deal with it and that is why you're seeing it."

Flashbacks in Post-Traumatic Stress Disorder: Surviving the Flood

I continue to explain as I enter high school he is a senior and he has people harassing me. I try to tell Mrs. Smith, my school counselor, about what happened with me and Bret. Nothing was done because I didn't remember the details of the rape. I just knew he raped me. I don't know if Mrs. Smith talked to him but somehow he finds out I talked about it.

Sandy responded, "She is bond to confidentiality. She couldn't have talked to him about it." I told her I know that but, "How did he find out?" I didn't tell anyone not even my mom, sisters, or my best friend. I kept it to myself until I talked with Mrs. Smith.

Bret has a boy shove me against a locker. Then he punches his fist next to my head and states, "This is for what you said about Bret." As a reflex and trying to defend myself, I punch him in the nose and he runs away with his hand over his bleeding nose. Out of the corner of my eye, I see my English teacher and fear that I am in trouble but instead he looks straight up in the air and goes into his classroom as if he didn't see a thing.

I then explain that after Bret rapes me he begins to bring young girls that have similar characteristics to my workplace, as if to show me who will be next. Each time he finds me; I quit my job and move on until he finds me again. This obsession with keeping me in fear of him becomes extreme when he slit my tires with a knife at my workplace. After work, I go out to my car and see what he did. As I am panicked and paranoia set in, I look around the parking lot while turning myself in circles making sure I don't miss an angle where he can have the advantage for another attack. I am terrified he will rape me again or kill me like he said he would do if I talked.

Then I begin to date another boy named, Tod. He was a tall, slender, brownish hair guy and he is very shy. He likes to play guitar and I think he is cool. One night as we are in his bedroom talking, there is a knock at the door. As we went to answer the door, to my surprise, it was Bret. My heart falls as Bret asks, "What is she doing here?" Tod explains that I am his new girlfriend. I retreat down to Tod's room in a panic and try to think what to say or do to get out of there. I hear the door shut and Tod comes back in his room. I ask, "How do you know Bret!" Tod replies, "He is my cousin." I really begin to panic. I wait for a while making small talk with Tod until I think Bret is gone and then I tell Tod it is late and I have to go home.

It is around 11:00 p.m. It is raining and I have to ride my bike home. I cautiously open the door and peek out in all the different directions and angles to ensure I wasn't going to be viciously attacked. I run to my bike and pedal as fast as I can in the dark with limited street lights. I am two blocks away from my house when I am on the side walk crossing the street from one curb to the next.

Then I see the black truck's head lights as I pray for God to keep me safe and protected. I black out and when I awake I am on the wet ground tangled in my bike. The driver is not even out of his truck yet, and when he opens his door he slowly walks up to me in a calm way. I know then it was Bret that had him do it because if I would have hit someone, I would be panicking and asking if the person was okay. He is trying to move me when Joe runs out of his house and tells him to leave me alone and that he called 911. There was another man beside me in a brown coat taking my information down while keeping me calm. There was also a construction worker directing traffic with a bright orange vest on but there was no traffic. The driver keeps trying to convince me to get up so he can move his truck so another car doesn't hit me. But Joe wouldn't let him. Joe knew me because I was his paper carrier when I was 12 years old. When the ambulance arrives, Joe tells them he will run and get my parents. When my parents arrive on the scene, the guy in the brown coat and the construction worker disappear into thin air. I know then that those were my guardian angels because I asked for God's protection.

The police ask me the same questions as the guy in the brown coat. They also want to know the direction I was going. I tell them and they are in disbelief that the car hit me that hard to turn me and my bike around in the opposite direction. I was taken to the hospital and released the same night. The ER doctor said, "I had a broken ankle and will be very sore the next day." He also gives my parents referrals to a bone doctor and a physical therapist.

Flashbacks in Post-Traumatic Stress Disorder: Surviving the Flood

The next day I can hardly breathe because my chest hurt so bad that I have to hold a pillow against my chest to help with the discomfort. I immediately call the attendance office at school to tell them what happened to me. To my surprise, they already knew as the attendance lady says, "Bret told the students in the lunch room that he is responsible and the guy didn't do the job right because you should have been killed."

I ask if she told Officer Jon and she replies, "Yes!" but his reply to her was that "People say things everyday they don't mean." I hang up the phone with her and in the evening attempt to call Tod and I ask, him "Did Bret do this to me?" He refuses to talk to me and tells me not to call again. Then I really knew he did it. Then suddenly I remember a few days prior. I am walking back from the store with my mom and a black truck is coasting beside us as we walk. My mom yells, "Run, honey, run, I think we are going to be taken!" I run leaving my mother behind and reach my house safely as the black truck drives right pass me while squealing the tires. It all makes sense that Bret was probably showing the guy who to hit and they planned this accident out carefully. That is when I knew I have to be careful in my everyday life, to stay on guard and never to let my guard down or Bret will have another chance to kill me.

Then when I have two daughters I get worse with worrying that he will abduct, rape, or kill them. So I become an overly protective mom not letting them be with their friends and have a normal life because of the fear that Bret will find them. When I try to take my guard down and let them have fun, something always reconfirmed that I need to keep my girls safe.

Sandy asked again, "Did your mom and dad call the police?" "I replied, "No, because I didn't tell them about the rape, stalking or the connection of the truck accident because I was so scared of what they would think of me." I remembered about my sister being called a slut, a fucking bitch, whore, when they found out she had sex at the age of 16 years old and I was only 14 years old. We ended the session at this point because I was exhausted and needed to stop.

Before I left, Sandy said, with a serious and calm voice while reflecting a concerned look on her face, "I think it is time to get a psychiatrist because I think you need medication to help manage your PTSD. I am worried for you." I told her I was scared for myself and worried about my family because they are seeing me constantly triggered and crying and it is starting to affect my entire life. I agreed I would go see Dr. Anderson for a referral to a psychiatrist.

Part Two
Abuse Turned Inward

Chapter 8
Submerged in Water

I was hired for my first job at 16 years old. I needed to support myself with food and clothing because my parents were struggling to raise us. As I worked long hours on the weekends, I started to notice this guy. He was skinny, had glasses, tall, and had long dark hair. His name was Scott. He was very cute and I wanted to ask him out but didn't have the courage. We lived close to each other so he walked me home after closing time. During one of those walks he finally asked me out. He warned me that he was 19 years old and in college but that didn't bother me.

We went to his house to watch his roommates practice songs for their band performances. About six month later, we decided to move in with each other. My mom and dad stopped fighting with me at this point, but they felt better because my sister, Andie, would be living with us. We rented a two bedroom apartment and we all contributed to the rent. By the time I was 17 years old, Scott decided that he wanted to go to graduate school. I was still in high school so I couldn't go with him so he broke up with me. It was a horrible break up because we had plans to get married and build a house on the land that his dad bought us. I felt abandoned.

I was heartbroken because I was alone again. This is when I gave up on myself and started to have random sexual relationships while trying to find Mr. Right. I ended up abusing myself.

I felt if I couldn't have Scott then nothing mattered anymore. I believed I wasn't worth caring about. I would stay out late and sometimes wouldn't come home. I would worry my parents because I had to move back in with them after Scott left because I couldn't afford the rent.

Then I bought a CB radio for my car and my behavior spun out of control because I would meet guys and put myself in danger by going to meet them. It seemed dangerous and naughty all at the same time and of course, I had friends that were doing the same thing. So here I am driving around town with friends in my car and we all had CB handles mine was "lonely heart." All the guys seemed to like that one. I met a lot of guys interested in meeting lonely heart because they felt they could solve her problem of being lonely.

Mike—I degraded myself as I let him take me to a high school hang out and had sex in the car. Then I was with him as we had sex in the shower at his house and his mother walked in on us. She was devastated and worried about her son getting me pregnant. Later, I found out that she was dying of cancer and he was acting out and trying to find love to numb his pain.

Gary—I was with friends at a party and everyone was drinking and having a great time. He was my sister's best friend and she really cared about him. I gave into peer pressure as it was announced that he was a virgin. He and friends wanted me to make him a man. I thought he wanted to have sex with me because he liked me, but after having sex with him that was all he wanted. He went out into the living room in front of everyone acting like he is the man and asked, "Who is next?" I felt dirty and disappointed because I really liked him. What made it worse; he promised not to tell my sister, Victoria, but he did and it hurt her deeply because they were such good friends and she had feelings for him.

Mickey—Then I met Mickey who was in the army on the weekends. He seemed like a really nice guy. He took me out to a restaurant, that I could never afford, and opened doors for me and really treated me with respect. His parents were nice as I met them before going out for dinner. We ended up having sex at the end of the night and I had a scare because the condom we were using broke. I was so scared about being pregnant that I counted the days until I had my period. Thank God I wasn't pregnant.

Bob—I met Bob, a semi-driver. I thought he was cool because he was a lot older than me. We drove in the middle of a winter storm with just the front end of the semi because we were on the way to pick up his load for his next trip out. The roads were icy and we almost had an accident a few times but thank God we got home safely. I had sex with him because I didn't' really care about myself. I felt numb. I was used to guys using me so it just didn't matter anymore. I never saw him again after that night.

Donny—I met Donny at one of our parties with friends again, everyone was drinking. He really acted like he cared because I started to tell him about my problems and he talked about his too. He seemed so compassionate and nice but he ended up like the rest. He just wanted to have sex because afterward he went home and I never saw him again.

Randy—Then one night I met Randy and he said, "After being with me "Lonely Heart", you will never be left lonely ever again." There were girls on the radio calling me a slut and a whore. I didn't feel that way because in my mind I was just trying to find someone to love me. I had all of my friends in my car rooting me on telling me to go meet him; so of course, I did because that is what Lonely Heart's reputation had become. Lonely Heart doesn't back down from a challenge that her friends put in front of her.

I went to meet Randy and we talked for hours and he was really nice. We did end up having sex but this time it was different because he took time with me and made sure I was comfortable. I felt love and excitement while being nervous because he made me feel something I never felt before. That was when I had my first orgasm during sex. I thought that meant I loved him. I was so excited and I hoped this time would be different and that he would stay with me.

Well this time it was different we ended up falling in love. We were both searching for something and thought we found it in each other. We dated for a while and then decided to have a baby together. Within a few months, I found out I was pregnant. Reality hits when I had to tell my mom that I was pregnant and I saw how devastated she was. My father was angry and my sisters were worried about me. The consequences of my actions finally reached me but it was too late. I was a junior in high school and now having a baby. We got married when I was five months pregnant at the courthouse.

The friends that were in the car with me all of those nights were suddenly not my friends anymore. They joined in with the rest of the school and treated me like an outcast. I was a slut, whore, bitch, believe me I heard it all. I no longer liked school. The only thing that helped me get through it was my parenting class. It helped me to express my feelings. I had peers in class just like me that were scared about their choices and learned what it meant to be pregnant. The teacher was nice and comforted us. We saw videos of the birth, parenting and how to involve our partner in the pregnancy. For some of the girls, their partners already left. I felt lucky that I had a husband for my baby.

By the time Sabrina was born, Randy didn't want anything to do with her. He wouldn't feed her, bathe her or even hold her. I was so angry because I tried to be the responsible mother. He left the house anytime he felt like it to go play pool and be with his friends while I stayed home with the baby.

I tried to force him to help me and he responded in anger while punching holes in the walls. I found myself in an abusive relationship, three months after Sabrina was born, with no one to turn to because my decisions landed me here. I felt it was my fault and I would just have to deal with it. With each argument he treated me like all I was good for was sex and pleasuring him. I fell deeply into depression. There would be days where I felt he was changing into a good guy again because he would help me or bring me flowers and act like he loved me again but would change back quickly.

I prayed each time he took my body against my will that God would stop him. When it kept happening, I was convinced that God has abandoned me and that I was being punished for being a slut and whore. I no longer stuck up for myself. I just let him do what he wanted because I was tired and had to go to school each morning and had to take care of the baby. I told myself that I wasn't going to drop out of school. I needed to finish because even though he would call me too stupid for college, I still wanted to go to college someday.

Finally the happy day arrived, I graduated from high school and everyone was happy, even my husband. I felt so much pride, accomplishment, and happiness. I felt I could do anything but it was short lived. The feelings of being trapped came up more strongly and I never told anyone how he treated me, not even my parents or sisters. He was excellent at looking like a good neighbor and husband when he had eyes on him. But at home, he was abusive and neglectful and would injure Sabrina. He would tell me it was an accident but I didn't believe him.

Then when I was 21, I really thought I was getting my husband to see what he was doing to me was wrong. He started to be nice to me and helped me with Sabrina but that was to only talk me into having another baby with him. After he knew I was pregnant, he changed back to the angry Randy that intimidated me and made me fearful that he would hurt me while I was pregnant too.

When Victoria was born it was supposed to be a joyous occasion, but it wasn't because the way Randy acted in the delivery room. When she wasn't a boy he became angry and as my mom saw his face turn red she started to yell, "What is wrong with you? Aren't you happy you have a healthy baby girl?" I looked at him and the machines that monitored my blood pressure went off. At this point, the nurse told me to calm down or I would have a stroke. I listened to her as I turned my head away weeping as the nurse softly rubbed my hand and as Randy was escorted out of my room.

I finally decided to get a divorce after Veronica was eight weeks old and Randy went to the pool hall instead of being with us in the hospital. Veronica had bronchitis. She had trouble breathing and needed to be on oxygen and was vomiting.

I have gone to the abuse center because I felt confused and felt abused but needed them to confirm it. Randy was good at making me think that I was crazy or depressed, because of the pregnancy. He reassured me that what he was doing wasn't abuse but in my heart I knew it was. After I explained how he treated me sexually and Sabrina's "accidents." The abuse center confirmed that I was being abused and needed to leave. They explained, as her mother, I would be held accountable if Sabrina was seriously injured by Randy. They asked if I had a safe place to go and I told them I would go to my parent house. I felt safe there as I filed for a divorce.

Part Three
Unconditional Love

Chapter 9
Life Preserver

I was trying to heal while I got my life on track and went to a technical college but I was lonely. One night I prayed for God to help me to find someone to love when I was ready. I asked him to send me a loving, kind, and gentle man who would accept that I have two daughters.

I graduated from the technical college and on Monday, I was on my way to work at the nursing home. I had been working there but since I graduated, it was my first day in my new position as administrative assistant. I was so excited I could hardly wait.

When I walked into the door, I was taken downstairs into the basement to my new office. I was starting to get acclimated to my new environment when I noticed a new maintenance man. He had light brown hair, short and was skinny and was wearing a black tight shirt with a pocket on the right side, which showed his muscular chest and arms. He had a nice tight butt. He walked with confidence with his chest and arms stuck out like a peacock proud of his feathers. I would see him coming down the hallway with his tool belt and I just felt like melting.

I wanted to know his name and I wanted to meet him. I hoped he would notice me. When I saw him punching out at the time clock for weeks, I would rush and punch out behind him hoping he would talk to me but he didn't. It was my horrible luck that this gorgeous guy was shy I, who am never shy, was finally speechless. My sisters would laugh because I am a talker usually.

I went over to my coworker, Casey, and I started to talk about the cute maintenance man and as I talked he was walking down the hallway. She stated loudly and pointed, "Oh you mean Ramone!" I said, "SH SH SH, he can probably hear you." As he walked passed us, he looked at us standing there looking at him. When his eyes met mine, I felt like I was going to faint. I told her, "I don't know what is coming over me. I have never felt this way before. I am shy and excited every time I see him. I feel like I could pounce on the poor little guy." Casey laughed and said, "It sounds like someone has a crush." I replied, "Sh Sh now, I will see you later," as I got back to work.

I continued talking for weeks about him. We were standing in Casey's office as I saw him coming our way I began to panic. Casey told me to act normal. As Ramone entered the room, he said, "Casey, did you need me to fix that wheelchair?" She replied, "Yes, it is over there but first I want you to meet Leslie. She is the new administrative assistant." I stood there speechless for a moment as he glanced into my eyes and said, "My name is Ramone." I replied, "Nice to meet you." Inside I could feel myself losing control. As he worked with his tool belt, I noticed how strong his hands looked." I suddenly, had to flee the office because I could feel myself blushing. Casey was laughing when she noticed me. I said, "Casey I will see you at lunch," I quickly excused myself and went back to my office.

At lunch I told Casey, "I can't get him out of my mind. He is all I think about at work, at home, in my sleep. Wow this has never happened to me before. He is so sexy I can't stand it." As Ramone walked by once again, I said, "Oh what I would love to do to him." Casey responded "Leslie!" "I apologize for my behavior but I can't stop thinking about him. I usually never date anyone from work but this time I have to make an exception."

My coworker blushed and said, "Okay, enough is enough, I can't listen to you anymore! I was having fun watching the two of you but too much information is being shared. I need to confess something to you. He is my uncle and from the way you are talking about him someday, you could be my aunt. Just so you know he has been asking about you too. Lucky me, you are both telling me how you want to meet but no one has the courage. He asked me how old you were and I told him you were a mature 23 years old. He is older than you." I replied, "I don't care." I looked at him and he is in great shape. I felt like I was buying a new used car but it still had the new car smell and it was still in great shape. I didn't care how old he was. She told me she would talk to him about asking me on a date. I was scared but agreed to let her.

That day I saw Ramone going to the time clock. I wanted to catch him to ask for a ride to the body repair shop to pick up my car. I was behind him and I taped him on the shoulder and said softly, "Ramone, can you give me a ride to the auto repair shop to pick up my car?" He replied cheerfully, "Sure!" We both walked out to his old truck quietly. The entire ride there, we both were quiet. I wanted to get to know him but didn't know what to say to him. I think he felt the same way because he was silent too. We finally arrived to pick up my car and then he says, "I'll see you tomorrow at work?" I told him, "Thank you for the ride. I look forward to seeing you tomorrow." As he drove away, I regretted not talking on the way over because that was my chance to get to know him a little.

The next day, I saw Ramone approaching me from the reflection in the TV. I was programming the internal TV station that the nursing home had. I acted like I didn't know he was there and then he spoke to me. He said softly, "Leslie," as he was looking down and shuffling his feet, If you are not busy on Saturday would you like to go with me to the comedy club?" I quickly spun around in my chair and said, "That would be great! Thank you for asking." He looked up with a smile on his face and said, "Okay I will pick you up at 5:00 p.m." I said, "Okay" and gave him my mother's address.

Saturday came and I was nervous. I tried on several outfits and wasn't sure what to wear. I ended up wearing tight jeans with a nice shirt. I had never been to the comedy club before and was looking forward to the show. It was a half an hour drive and it was already 5:00 p.m. I'm not sure when it starts. I kept looking out my mother's bedroom window for him. My mom said, "Leslie, sit down. He will come to the door." I replied, "Mom, he is late!" "How is that for a first date? He should have called me if he was going to be late." Just then I see his truck pulled up as I looked at the clock and it was 6:10 p.m. He knocked and I answered it, "Hi, my parents would like to meet you if that is okay." He seemed nervous as he walked into the living room. He said, "Hi, my name is Ramone. Leslie and I work together," as he firmly shook my dad's hand. I decided at that moment to forgive him for being late because he seemed like a nice gentleman.

He opened the door for me and as I walked down the walkway, he ran in front of me to open the truck door as well. Wow, a real gentleman. I have never been treated with so much respect. I couldn't help but think he had the night planned and I bet we end up at his place. We'll see if he is a jerk or not.

On the way, I was so nervous and I didn't want dead air so I talked the entire way there. I made sure I told him up front that I am a divorced woman with two little girls ages 2 and 4. I told him about my parents and anything else I could think of. I felt out of breath a lot of the time but he just listened and smiled at me.

We finally got to the comedy club and the guy at the door asked for our tickets. Ramone asked, "You mean we can't buy them at the door?" The guy answered, "No, sorry we have a full house tonight." As the people behind us moved forward, Ramone apologized to me. I felt very disappointed and embarrassed. I kept thinking to myself. Why didn't he buy tickets ahead of time especially if he planned on going on a date? How

Flashbacks in Post-Traumatic Stress Disorder: Surviving the Flood

embarrassing for him. We decided to go to the movie theater to see what was playing.

We decided to go to a movie called *Scary Movie*, but it was a comedy. We walked up to the ticket booth and to my surprise he paid for us. Then we went to the concession stand and I pulled some money out and he insisted on paying. I always get a big soda and popcorn. The movie had some sexual scenes and I knew I blushed from time to time. I wondered if he noticed because we were sitting where there was a little light. As he looked at me, I took the focus off of me by commenting on the two kids in front of us and stated, "They don't look old enough to be seeing this movie." Ramone agreed.

I put my hand on the hand rest and wanted to see if he would hold my hand and he did but he moved my hand onto his lap because he said it was more comfortable. I kept thinking. Is he going to be a creep or a nice guy? I have had my share of creeps who think of themselves so I am praying really hard for a nice one.

When the movie was over we started home. I was more relaxed this time and I was able to give him a chance to talk about himself. I noticed we were getting close to town so I asked, "Where are we going?" He said, "I don't know." "Where do you want to go?" I replied, "I am not sure but I am not ready to go home." Believe it or not we decided to see another movie and again he paid. We saw "*Autumn in New York*", which was about a younger girl dating an older guy. It fit us just right. It was a tear jerker because she got sick and she dies in the end. Of course I was crying, I couldn't help it. This gave him the opportunity to put his arms around me to comfort me and it felt nice.

Then it was time to go home and I really didn't want the date to end. We just finally began talking and getting comfortable with each other. When we reached my parents house, he asked if I wanted him to walk me to the door and I said, "No, but just wait a minute." I got out of the truck and went over to his side as we kept talking and holding hands. I really didn't want this night to end because maybe he wouldn't want a second date. I finally had to say good-bye but before I went in, it was like magic. We both wanted a kiss as we both started to move towards each other. Wow, this kiss was the best kiss I have ever experienced. He had his hands on the side of my face as he passionately kissed me with his warm, soft lips but still gave me the opportunity to take the lead as well. I didn't want to stop but I had to go into the house.

I thanked him for the wonderful night and he said, "We should do this again." I said, "Yes, when?" He told me he would call me. There you go, he will call me. Will he really call me? As he left, I felt so hot and excited inside. I was as light as a feather. I watched as he left and hoped to God that this was not a sick joke and that I wouldn't get my heart broken. I have had it happen to me several times.

The next day I woke up early and I waited and no call by 12:00 p.m. so I called him. He sounded happy to hear my voice as he said, "Hi Leslie!" "How are you today?" I told him good and repeated what I told him the night before, how much fun I had and that I would like to see him again. He sounded surprised that I would like a second date with him. We planned it for the next day because his brother was in town.

We volunteered to do a brat fry where we grilled brats, hotdogs, and hamburgers for charity. As we worked the booth, I was the cash handler and he was the griller. I couldn't stop looking at him and he couldn't stop staring at me. I felt so attracted to him but I kept remembering to take this relationship slow because all my prior experiences with guys was once you have sex they leave. After the brat fry, I told Ramone that I couldn't go out with him because my two year old daughter, Veronica, was very ill. I explained that I took her to the doctor but they wouldn't do anything about her bad breathing. Her sides were caving in and my mom and I were worried because she had bronchitis and was so small.

I was surprised because Ramone didn't have children but he seemed to be very concerned. He said, "I'll take you to another hospital for a second opinion." I said, "Really, where?" It was again a 30 minute drive but he wanted to help my daughter. We decided to pick her up at my mom's house. Ramone waited in the truck as I went and got Veronica and her car seat. As Ramone was putting the car seat in the car, was when my sister, Victoria, came out of the house yelling at me saying, "No one is going to want to be your doctor, if you don't trust them. Why do you trust a guy you just met? He is too old for you!"

We finally got into the truck and drove away leaving my sister in the dust. He looked at me with sadness in his eyes as he said, "She is right you know. I shouldn't be with you. I am too old for you." I said, "I knew this would come up so let's get it out of the way. How old are you?" I was thinking 35 years old but he looked at me and said, "I am 43 years old." Well, that was older than I thought, a 20 year difference, but he looked like he was 30 years old. I said, "It doesn't matter to me because I have dated many assholes in my life and they were my age. I have decided to date you because I want to see where this relationship goes. Is that okay with you, Ramone?" He smiled and said, "Yes, that is okay with me." I felt bad because my sister was unkind to him. I apologized for my sister and explained she is just worried about me because of my past decisions. He told me he understood she was just trying to be a big sister.

When we got to the hospital he took me to the emergency room with Veronica and the doctor examined her. He said, "It is good that you brought her in because she is having hard time breathing." He pulled up her gown and we saw her chest caving in too far. The doctor said, "She needs breathing treatments to open her airway up." I explained that we went to the hospital in town and he asked me which doctor because he will make a complaint for us. He discharged us and prescribed a nebulizer which we had to rent at another location. After we went to get the nebulizer and medication, Ramone took us home. He helped me and Veronica into the house and stayed by my side as I explained to my mom what the doctor said. My mom was relieved as Ramone took a seat next to my dad and began a conversation about what he was watching on TV, the Vietnam War on the history channel.

I was amazed at how much Ramone knew about the subject and my dad seemed happy to have someone to talk to about it. Ramone excused himself as it was getting late. I walked him to the door and gave him a kiss. He said, "I will check on you two tomorrow."

After he left my mom said, "Okay, how old is he?" He seems to know too much in your dad's and my age group." I said, "Do you like him?" They both answered, "Yes." I said, "I will let you get to know him and then I will tell you. Mom, his kisses are so passionate," as my dad exited to the kitchen until us girls were done talking.

The next day Ramone did just what he said. He called to check up on us. My mother said, "Go somewhere with him. It's okay. I will watch Veronica." Ramone picked me up and we drove to his place. I was really nervous. He wanted me to meet his partner, his dog, Buddy. As soon as we got there, Ramone let Buddy out of the house and he ran and ran without a leash. He ran so fast that he was out of sight. When Ramone called for him he came back quickly and was very playful. I could tell he cared a lot for his dog.

Ramone lived on a channel of water and the sun began to go down. I was admiring the view when he came up behind me and wrapped his strong arms around me tightly swaying me back and forth gently, as we enjoyed the sunset. I replied, "It has been a long time since anyone has touched me like this. I told him, "I miss feeling loved." Just then he said,

"Everyone should feel loved," as he led me into the house and into his bedroom. I was thinking here goes. I expected him to want sex but he didn't. He gently laid me down and told me to turn around and as I did what he said, he put his arms around me while spooning me. He asked, "Why don't you feel loved?" I shared my life story with him and felt comfortable with him. He just held me and talked to me all night not expecting a thing. It was then that I decided I wanted to be his wife. If I could have a man respect me like he did, I wouldn't ask God for any more favors because I would be set for life."

I went to go visit my sister, Andie, in New York for a week. We missed each other so much we called each other every night. When I got home, Ramone and I decided to move in together with my two girls. He accepted these little girls as if they were his own. He even dealt with the fact I had an abusive ex-husband and he treated him with respect when he came to pick up Sabrina. Veronica had two years of watching her dad take Sabrina before he took her because she wasn't potty trained. Ramone would have special time with Veronica when Sabrina was gone.

We dated for three years and he finally asked me to marry him. He took me to a restaurant and asked me to marry him without a ring because he wanted me to pick it out. After dinner, we went and picked it out together. I was excited to show everyone. I couldn't have been happier. I wanted a big wedding so I started to plan right away. We ended up having an outdoor wedding at an art museum and had 300 guests. Ramone had a huge family and we both had a lot of friends to invite. We had our reception at a hotel. The only thing that could have made it better was if his parents were still alive. However, we did honor them with a memorial candle at our wedding and before we went to our reception, we paid our respects as a family to their gravesite.

At our wedding, I spoke of how gentle and kind-hearted my husband was. I knew again that he was the man of my dreams when I heard how he sacrificed his life for his 1st grade school teacher. She became ill while he was in high school. Ramone shopped for her, maintained her lawn, cleaned her house, ran errands and looked after her so she could stay living in her home. She passed away 22 years later. He also took care of his father with Alzheimers and his mother who passed away from a stroke.

He also watched over his aunt who was in a nursing home with Alzheimers where we both worked at that time. One day she asked for Ramone to come see her. She forgot her daughter and other family members but never Ramone. She always knew him. She glanced sadly at Ramone and said, "Honey, I don't think I will make that dance." She was referring to the dance at our wedding. We knew she was dying. Ramone said cheerfully, "Well that is okay," as he moved the tables out of the way in the kitchen area. Then he took her in his arms and said, "May I have this dance?" She was delighted. I watched in tears and loved Ramone even more because he was so kind and loving to her. Shortly after the dance, a few weeks later, his aunt passed away. I will never forget how happy Ramone made her because he made her last wish come true by dancing with her. I knew if anything happened to me, he would stay with me and would never abandon me.

We shared many happy memories with the girls. Ramone took the girls on nature walks while showing them how to track animals. He taught the girls how to survive in the wilderness by making a hut made of sticks, leaves, and mud. He also demonstrated how to make a fire with a special stick with no matches.

He also had a love for animals. If he found a wounded animal he would try to rescue it by trapping it and bringing it to the vet, nature reserve or by calling the DNR. If an animal was hit on the highway where we lived, he would take a shovel and would give the animal a proper burial in the woods we owned. This was Ramone's way of giving the animal's spirit back to God. The girls would help him by saying a special prayer and put flowers down for the animals, mostly feral cats. This taught our daughters to have respect for every living thing.

Our happiness started to be shaken as I was unable to cope with my PTSD, conversion, and somatization disorders. As the flashbacks, body memories became too much for me, I began to change. I would be irritable and would yell a lot but wasn't sure why. When I finally got help, it was a God-sent.

I know now that God gave me a good man so I could handle going through the healing process while making Ramone strong enough to support me. He had patience and compassion for what I went through. It has made us stronger together as a family. I hope someday I find something that I can give Ramone that will measure up to what he has done for me.

Chapter 10
A Child Was Born

It was a nice and quiet evening with just Ramone and me. We decided rather than go out for date night we would stay home and watch a movie. Ramone asked me to pick the movie. I was browsing our collection when I came across our wedding video. I said, "How about our wedding video? We haven't seen it for a long time." Ramone replied, "That's a great idea!"

We got comfortable on the sofa while cuddling under a warm blanket. As we watched the video, I became emotional because it was such a beautiful wedding. I finally had the man of my dreams who would never hurt or leave me and he accepted my daughters as his own. We continued to watch the wedding, ceremony, then the reception toasts. I was surprised because I forgot that Casey and her husband and many others left messages for our future, as husband and wife.

Casey and her husband's message made me laugh because I was trying for years to get Ramone to have a baby with me but he felt he was too old. When we met he was 43 years old and he was 47 years old when we got married. I was only 23 years old and when married I was 27. He still said he didn't want to have a baby. He had fears of the child calling him grandpa or having his child be embarrassed by him because of his age. I finally gave up on this discussion and respected Ramone's decision not to have another child.

When we saw Casey's message it brought back memories on how she was the one responsible for getting us together. I laughed at how silly and shy we were and felt without her help we wouldn't have ever had that first date. Her message to us was, "Come on Ramone have a baby with Leslie. Go for baby number three." His family always wanted Ramone to have a baby but he never found anyone until he found me. We both laughed at many other messages saying the same thing.

When we were finished watching the video, we decided to go to bed because Ramone had to work in the morning. Instead we lay in bed talking about how we got together and finally asking questions of each other. I asked him, "What did you think of me on our first date? Did you think what did I get myself into because of me talking the whole way to the movies?" Ramone replied, "I felt you were pretty and nice. I was happy you were talking because it took all the pressure off of me." We both laughed as we reminisced about how we got together.

Then out of nowhere Ramone asked, "Do you still want to have a baby with me?" I said, "Yes, only if you really want one." He told me he has been thinking about it a lot lately and decided he wanted to have a child with me. Then he had a big grin on his face as he asked, if I wanted to get started? With excitement and love in my heart, I said, "Let go for it!" It took a year to get pregnant but the day finally came. I took a pregnancy test and finally it was positive. I was so excited. I yelled, "Ramone, we are finally pregnant!" We were excited as he called his family and I called mine.

It was the first time I experienced love and support during a pregnancy. Ramone got excited when the baby kicked and concerned when my blood pressure rose. This was truly a beautiful and loving experience that I didn't experience with my ex-husband.

I continued to have symptoms of post-traumatic stress disorder but they were mistaken for being part of the pregnancy. Smells, sounds, and touch started to bother me all of a sudden. I figured that this was normal because I heard every pregnancy is different. I wasn't worried until the flashbacks and nightmares began. First, I had nightmares of the birth and when they handed me the baby, it had my rapist's head on it.

Then flashbacks of how my ex-husband would abuse me during my second pregnancy by threatening me harm. When he got mad he would yell and punch holes in the walls. He was obsessed with knowing the sex of the baby but our insurance didn't cover an ultrasound. He had to wait for the baby to be born. He became angry in the delivery room as they announced it was a girl. I had high blood pressure and the machines began beeping as I saw his expression of anger. My parents yelled at him because of the way he behaved, as he stared angrily at me and the baby. They yelled, "Aren't you happy you have another healthy baby girl?" He didn't say a word just kept staring at the baby with anger. My blood pressure rose to a dangerous level as the nurse took my hand and turned my face gently away from my ex-husband.

She explained very calmly that I had to calm down or I was going to have a stroke. She explained there was no time to administer medication to lower my blood pressure. I closed my eyes and prayed that I wouldn't have a stroke because I had to protect my baby from my ex-husband. My parents were worried for our safety as well as the nurses. They had him escorted out of the hospital. I tried to ignore the flashbacks and body memories and didn't tell Ramone the difficulties I was having. I wanted this to be a very happy experience for him to remember for the rest of his life.

The ninth month came and I was so ready to have the baby. I was on bed rest for three weeks because my blood pressure was dangerously high because of preeclampsia. I had this problem with all my pregnancies but this time it was the most serious for me and the baby.

Ramone and I were taking a nap in the evening when I felt the baby move strangely. I went to the bathroom and sat on the toilet. To my surprise, a large amount of water burst into the toilet and all over the floor. I yelled, "Ramone, I think my water broke." I was alarmed because this never happened with my other two pregnancies. I quickly found the phone and called the doctor as water is streaming down my legs. The doctor told me to calmly get ready. The baby was coming. Go to the hospital. He reassured me we had a lot of time to get to the hospital. I yelled a second time, "Ramone, get up, my water just broke!" Ramone ran out of the bedroom and asked, "Are you sure?" Then he saw the water trickling down my legs. Every time I moved my water broke further. He got my suitcase and me into the car. The other kids were spending the night at their dad's house. We decided not to call anyone and to have a private birth with just the two of us.

On the way to the hospital, my water kept breaking and I was amazed of how much water my body could hold. I glanced at Ramone as he concentrated on driving fast to the hospital. He repeatedly asked if I was okay as I kept my breathing up through contractions that were now coming every minute.

When we arrived at the hospital, he parked the car in front of the hospital entrance and ran in to get the nurses to help me. The loving concern he had was reflected by his facial expressions. I really felt loved and safe. I laughed because I was the only calm one because this was his first child and he didn't know what to expect.

We entered the birthing delivery unit and right away nurses were asking questions. I calmly answered them; Ramone stayed motionless observing the commotion.

As the nurses wheeled me to my room, my water continued breaking, as I apologize for the mess. They said, "That is okay this is all part of having a baby", as we laughed.

Because of my high blood pressure and preeclampsia, I was put in the bed right away and was hooked up to the baby and heart monitor, blood pressure machine, and also the nurses started an IV for the epidural. I was in really bad pain as we breathed through each contraction. It took two tries to put the epidural in and it ended up only working on one half of my body.

As it got closer to delivering the baby, the nurse told me that she called the doctor twice with no response. Ramone thought his job would be to videotape this wonderful experience for us. The nurse glanced at him, as I was ready for delivery. They were short-staffed and the doctor hasn't arrived yet. She calmly told Ramone to put the camcorder down. The nurse explained that he had to help her deliver the baby without the doctor. I looked at him as he had a panicked look on his face but agreed to help.

He held one of my legs as we together delivered our baby into the world. The doctor arrived in time to catch the baby. The moment that the baby was born the doctor said, "It a boy!" We were so overjoyed because he will be the last one to carry the Raddatz's name. We named him Kota. He was screaming and crying as they put him on my stomach. Ramone carefully cut the cord. As I looked into my son's eyes, I knew he was a very special little one. My husband was so overjoyed. They took Kota from us so the nurses could do their assessments. Ramone followed the nurses, watching the nurses nervously. Shortly, they returned him and said he scored perfectly. They told me he was a little blue and to warm him by placing him skin-against-skin. The nurse helped lay him on my chest. It was such a bonding experience as I saw how happy we were because this was the gift no one else could give him but me.

We both felt our family was complete and was happy as we started to call around to both of our families to announce our Kota's birth. My blood pressure stabilized and everything was perfect.

Part Four
Ex-husband's Abuse Surfaces

Chapter 11
Swim to the Surface

I was at work when I noticed I was zoning in and out, I couldn't concentrate at work. I did my breathing exercises and refocused my attention, as my counselor instructed me to do.

I finished the workday and called my husband, Ramone, and told him I was going to visit my mom and sister, Victoria. As I drove, I started to remember hurtful comments my ex-husband, Randy, said to my daughters and me. The hurt started to surface and tears began to flow freely. I struggled to restrain the tears by wiping my eyes while trying to maintain focus on driving. I reassured myself that I would be all right.

I was relieved as I safely pulled into my mother's driveway. At this point, my head was pounding with pain because of the overwhelming memories. My head felt like it was ready to explode. As I walked into the house, my mother greeted me with a smile. I rushed over to her and started to cry in her arms. I needed to feel the love and security of my mother.

She asked, "What happened?" "Is it work?" I replied "No!" I replied, "I am remembering things Randy would say to the girls and me." I explained the hurt I felt as I sobbed, "Mom, he was supposed to be my husband. He was supposed to love and protect me." "Instead he hurt Sabrina and me."

My mother did her best to comfort me. After a while, I was able to calm down enough to put Leslie's famous happy face on and went home to my family.

When I awoke the next morning, I felt an urgent need to find my poetry to share at my next therapy appointment. I looked for the poem called *"Home Alone"* which explained the intense fear I had when Ramone leaves the house but that wasn't all I found. I found an envelope and remembered sharing my writing with my sister, Andie.

I also found pages that detailed the abuse I endured at the hands of my ex-husband. As I read the pages, I was in disbelief of what I was reading. It was almost like I was reading something for the first time. The tears began to stream down my face as I started to see the images, and feel the emotions I felt back then. The memories resurfaced the feelings of not trusting my ex-husband with my daughters.

I was hard on myself as I was angry for not remembering what happened. I felt the guilt of not keeping my children safe from him. I remembered repeated attempts to tell the authorities when we went through mediation for his visitation after the divorce. I kept telling them that he couldn't be trusted as I explained what I went through with him and his temper. I also told them how I didn't have choices when it came to sex. I was concerned he would sexually abuse his daughters. I was told that didn't mean it would happen to the girls. The mediator told me, "You have to let him be a father. If anything happens he will suffer the consequences."

As more memories came I felt overwhelmed with sadness, and hopelessness. I panicked to find the phone. I dialed my sister, Andie. As I heard her voice answer "Hello," I struggled to hold back my tears as she asked, "How are you today?" My resistance released as I let myself be vulnerable with the loving voice and understanding of a sister.

As she listened, I could hear compassion and understanding in her voice. She reassured me that my feelings were normal and that it wouldn't last forever. The healing process that I was entering into is a hard journey but she was so happy that I have begun. She told me that she knew for years that I needed to start to let go of my trauma.

I explained the doubts and guilt I was feeling for the way I felt about my ex-husband. As Andie talked to me, she was able to put my mind at ease. She told me she remembered what I told her as I was experiencing it. She told me to trust my memories because they are right. She warned me that her battery on her phone was low and after a short time the phone was silent.

I felt better but as I entered my kitchen I became overwhelmed with having to clean the kitchen. I felt like time was running out and it was <u>Urgent</u>! I began to wash the dishes as my memories kept coming. Then a familiar feeling, I noticed my arms were folded while standing and I was rocking myself. Hopelessness came over me. I lost time as I stared blankly. When I snapped out of it, the memories came. This time I needed no therapeutic machines:

I had a memory of me rushing into the kitchen of my apartment with Randy to reassure myself it was clean. Then I had a memory of me sitting on my cold kitchen floor as I rocked back and forth feeling as if I wasn't safe with myself. Then the thought entered my mind to kill myself to escape, but it was replaced with remembering that my baby, Sabrina, needed me to protect her. I needed to be strong. I felt isolated and trapped as I struggled to breathe. I have failed in so many things in my life but this I vowed I would not screw up. When I heard Sabrina cry, I sprung back into mommy mode and everything was fine again.

After I was released from this flashback the tears returned and panic came rushing in. I reached out to my other sister, Victoria. Right away she answered and heard me crying hysterically as she asked, "Are you okay?" I responded, "No, I am having a bad day." She asked, "What happened?" I replied, "My memories, too many memories. I remember why I left Randy and why I don't trust him with the girls."

She reassured me that what I was experiencing would pass. Her voice was so calm and she reminded me to breathe slowly in and out as she demonstrated and told me to follow. Then she urged me to come over to talk in person. I just couldn't stop crying as more and more and more memories appeared.

I remembered my body not being mine. The control was taken by someone who was supposed to love and protect me, Randy. The first time control was lost I remember a feeling of disbelief and confusion because I felt violated, a familiar feeling from my past. I was raped when I was 14 years old by my boyfriend, Bret.

The comments Randy said to me started to echo in my ears as I tried desperately to block them from coming. My heart started to hurt as they broke through: "Women don't want to have sex with their husbands after they have babies."

He threatened to cheat on me if I didn't want to have sex with him. I was blamed for being too sexy or wearing the wrong clothes. He would get an erection and say it was my fault. I didn't do anything for this to occur. He said, "It was because I was too sexy." I tried to fix the problem by dressing down but it didn't work.

He made me feel that no one else would want me and I was lucky to have him. When I talked about going to college he would say that, "I was too stupid for college." When I wore makeup, I was accused of wanting to find someone else.

Then the memories of living in our first home came to me. *I remember feeling tired all the time. I was a mother, wife, and student in high school. I received no help at all. When my daughter would finally fall to sleep, I knew it wouldn't be a quiet night. My ex-husband would demand sex by kissing me as I said, "Not tonight, I'm tired." He would ignore me as he started to kiss my neck, as he pressed his penis and all his weight against my backside. He would say it was my fault for being too sexy. He would keep this up for hours if I let it. In the end, I would have to give the control of my body over to him so that I could sleep.*

Then another memory of the second home rushed into my head. I remember just laying there and letting Randy satisfy himself. There was no love, no emotion, just a feeling of defeat and sadness of being violated. I would redress myself and turn over and sob quietly because I was so deeply hurt. It was like he had no feelings of remorse at all. As I sobbed, I tried to be quiet because our second baby was asleep in the bassinette next to my side of the bed. As she would wake to be fed, I would check to see if he was asleep before I wouldn't dare breastfeed her in his presence.

When it came to breastfeeding he made me feel it was dirty and abusive to my first daughter. He told me that I would get aroused when the baby would suck on my breasts because that is what occurred when he did it. In fear of this reaction, I didn't breastfeed her.

When my second daughter was born and the nurse came in to ask what method I would use, I asked if I would be aroused by her feeding and she replied, "No." At that moment, I decided to breastfeed her because I wanted to experience this bond with her. I was careful to give myself a few moments to compose myself before feeding her in fear she could feel my emotions. I wanted for her to feel safe.

As I was still talking to my sister, I remembered going to an abuse center as an outpatient. I went there because I suspected that I was being abused but still doubted myself. He would make me feel crazy because he would tell me that it wasn't abuse that I was depressed. He had a right to have sex with his wife. He would injure our first daughter and tell me it was my fault. Everyone around us would witness him being a loving husband and a helpful neighbor. There were moments when I would experience this too, when I threatened to leave, but it always was short lived.

The counselor at the abuse center told me that my feelings were correct that he was abusing my daughter and me. She told me that perpetrators do a good job fooling loved ones around you because this makes you more helpless and more likely to stay with them. She explained the cycle of abuse and about the honeymoon stage. That explained why he would be nice to me for a short time and then would continue with his abuse.

I was isolated from my friends because he made it impossible for me to go anywhere. He didn't do babysitting, as he called it. I also didn't trust him alone after the incident with my first daughter, Sabrina:

I had fought with him to watch her. She was around two years old. When I got home I will never forget the image of him sitting on the couch as he said, "Go look at what your daughter did." In a panic, I rushed up the soft cushiony steps while thinking, "What did he do to her?" When I opened the door at first I didn't see her. Then I heard a soft cry "Mama" as she peered from behind the door with a helpless, fearful, at fault look on her tiny face as she reached up to me. I noticed a strong smell of poop as I looked at her she was covered in it. Her arms, legs, stomach, even in her teeth and on her bed. I remember thinking did my ex-husband do this to teach me not to leave the house or did she just get into her diaper?

I screamed down the stairs at him asking how long she was like this. I could tell by the way it was dried on her skin that it must have been a long time. He rushed up the stairs screaming as I rushed her into the bathroom and locked the door. I ran the water as I sang "The Rose" to her to try to drown out the noise. He punched the hollow door and made two holes in it.

I comforted her as I tried to hold back my tears because I felt it was my fault that this happened to her. I remember saying I was sorry over and over again and reassured her that I would never leave her with daddy again. As I tried to scrub her gently to remove the dried poop, I saw the red skin underneath. I couldn't imagine how bad this must have hurt her. As I smelled the overwhelming stench of poop, I started to vomit in the toilet while still trying to comfort her. When the poop was mostly off, I drain the water and replaced it with new water so I could rewash her again. I helped her clean her mouth out. I realized he had done this to squash my growing empowerment so I could return to my status below him.

Then we quietly left the bathroom and snuck into her room locking the door behind us. She sat in a towel as I cleaned and replaced her bed sheets, blankets, and pillow. I tried to clean up the mess on the wall and carpet the best I could without having to leave the room. I put lotion on Sabrina's skin and redressed her and wrapped her up in her blanket as I sang her "The Rose," again.

After she fell asleep, I stayed with her and slept too. I had my head on her bed next to hers with my body slouched on the floor because her bed was a small toddler bed.

After this memory, I felt an overwhelming panic and need to get my records to again validate my feeling now in the present. I hung up with my sister so I could call the abuse center. I was disappointed to find out that they only kept records for 10 years. I wasn't able to get the validation I needed, but had the satisfaction of remembering that they did validate me 13 years ago.

Part Five
Darkness into the Light

Chapter 12
God's Love

My relationship with God consisted of me praying at home in private. I didn't belong to a church because I didn't grow up in a religious home. I thought that if you didn't go through the religion classes as a child that it was too late to join a church, I accepted that this was it.

I wanted to believe that God was with me because I wouldn't have survived my childhood if he wasn't looking out for me. However, I struggled with why I had to suffer so much in my life. I knew there was a plan but I just wish I knew it so I could see the suffering coming to an end.

In 2003 God led me on the path to change my job. I became the secretary for a religious organization. I had no idea how this would work out because not only do I not belong to a church, but also I didn't know anything about religious life.

I trusted in God and he helped me to work full-time as I also went to night classes to get two bachelors and to care for my daughter, Sabrina, with epilepsy. It was very difficult because her seizures could occur at any time. I would have to rush her to the emergency room each time she had a seizure because doctors had to administer valium to get her out of her seizure. I felt comforted while in college because Ramone knew how to take care of her because his brother had seizures too. God helped me with many obstacles in my life as the odds kept stacking up against me. The difference with this period in my life is I had my coworkers' prayer support which helped me feel the gift of prayer, love, and compassion.

As the years went by, I still felt guilty because I was afraid if the religious organization I worked for knew I didn't belong to a church that they wouldn't like me anymore. I tried a few different churches with my sister, Victoria, but I just didn't feel at home with them.

There was a certain coworker who I think knew because while I was working in the workroom she said in a gentle and soft voice, "Leslie, I think you have been searching for something for a long time." She laid a booklet down on the counter as she explained that there were adult religion classes being offered at a local catholic church. She also told me about the children's program. I was so excited it felt like a heavy load was lifted off my shoulders because I explained to her that I thought it was too late for my family to join a church. She reassured me that God loves me and it is never too late. She shared her story of being in a different religion before changing her religion and her experience as she transitioned into becoming catholic. She left me with the booklet and my thoughts.

I pondered on it for a while and decided to go to a class to try it out. My husband came with me and I was excited but scared. The first night I could tell this would be a good fit because everyone was loving and inviting. They already accepted me and they didn't even know me. They explained the process of becoming catholic. I was surprised that they weren't pushy about joining. They wanted you to join only if you felt the call to.

As I entered the chapel for the first time, I felt the overwhelming presence of God. I knew God was with me because I felt God's love and compassion for me. Tears welled up in my eyes and my heart was heavy with darkness, pain, guilt, and regret for how I lived my life. I couldn't stop crying because finally I knew without a doubt that God didn't abandon me and that he had a plan for me. Everything would be revealed to me at the right time, not my time, but God's time.

Flashbacks in Post-Traumatic Stress Disorder: Surviving the Flood

As the choir started to sing, I looked at the beautiful stained glass and saw the sunlight shining through and a feeling of hope, love, and clarity came over me, as I felt strong and like I had a purpose because God held me safely in his arms, like a father protecting his daughter from harm. The never-ending search for love was over because I finally found it.

This is when I felt the transition of stepping from the darkness and into the light. I realized God's love was with me all the time but I didn't see it because I was too busy just trying to survive. I let the darkness; sin and guilt keep me from God's love and protection. I felt like the lost lamb and God took his time to repeatedly try to reach me by showing me he was present. I was blind until this moment.

My healing began at my family and my baptism. We all kneeled together in the baptismal fount and were introduced to the church. As we heard our names and the blessing spoken by the Father, I quickly prayed for God to accept me and forgive me for all my sins.

It was at that moment, I felt the holy water trickled down my face and a layer of weight was lifted from my shoulders. My heart felt a little lighter and I realized with God's help I could be released from the rest of the weight, if I asked for help. My entire life I didn't ask for help. I depended on myself in fear that I would just be a victim of more abuse and disappointment.

I decided that this was the time to take a leap of faith and ask God for help. As I glanced at the Stations of the Cross and reflected on God's life I realized God suffered for our sins and so must I suffer for mine to achieve freedom. As I reflected on the Stations of the Cross I could only imagine the suffering Mother Mary went through as she watched her son being crucified. I prayed for Mother Mary's protection, love and wisdom to help my children and me through all the sexual abuse and trauma that we experienced in our lives. I prayed for God to give me strength, courage and mercy to get through another chapter in my life.

I knew this would be the hardest chapter because I had to review my entire life and experience the suffering again. But then I could surrender completely to God to be healed in my mind, body and spirit. I knew that there were many paths to God and peace but I had to find a way for me.

Part Six
Admission to a Psychiatric Unit

Chapter 13
Out of Control Crisis Care

It was a sunny day and as Sandy suggested a few days prior, I made an appointment with my primary doctor, Dr. Anderson, to get a referral for a psychiatrist.

While driving, I felt dizzy and zoned out. I finally reached the clinic and parked. The "child within" surfaced. I felt panic, scared, and unsafe and my heart began beating out of control. I got out of my van slowly and walked towards the front door.

A man opened the door and held it open with a smile as he greeted me good morning. When I stepped through the door and entered the lobby, I felt paranoid. I approached the receptionist and said, "My name is Leslie Raddatz, here to see Dr. Anderson." She replied, "Honey, you need to speak up. I can't hear you." I tried again but still not loud enough. The "child within" thought she was in trouble and was ashamed for not being able to control her emotions. The anxiety took over. I finally was able to raise my voice loud enough for her to hear me. She told me to sit down, as the doctor would be right with me.

I glanced at the lady sitting across from me. I gave her a reassuring smile that I was okay. I couldn't help but stare at her because she reminded me of my deceased grandmother, Angelica. The "child within" wished her grandmother was here to help her through this but instead she sat all alone like she has done her entire life. I heard my name from a distance and then louder the second time as I was zoning out again. I slowly stood up and walked hesitantly towards the nurse. She asked, "How is your day today?" but I was unable to move my lips to answer because I was slipping away.

As we sat down she asked routine questions like, "Why are you being seen today?" I explained that my therapist, Sandy, suggested it was time for a referral to a psychiatrist because the Paxil wasn't working. Then she asked, "What are your symptoms?" I felt ashamed as I told her I had PTSD (Post-traumatic stress disorder) which includes dizziness, zoning out and that the flashbacks (memories) are coming too fast. My body is experiencing the pain of my abuse as if it is still happening today!

The nurse took my vitals and appeared concerned as she told me, "Your blood pressure is 142/118 which is too high!" I asked, "How can that be? I am on blood pressure pills to lower my blood pressure."

A general practitioner, Dr. Anderson, entered and sat down next to me, as he calmly asked, "What can I do for you?" My adult self surfaced as I explained, "I am being treated for PTSD and the symptoms are out of control." I said, "I am dizzy and feel emotionally unstable and I am also zoning out while driving." He said, "The dizziness is probably because your blood pressure is too high." "I can fix that by prescribing you an additional blood pressure pill," as he pulled up my records in the computer and sent the prescription to the pharmacy. Then he turned back to me, "What other symptoms are you experiencing?" I said, "I have been in intense therapy with Sandy at the *New Beginnings Counseling Center* since March. I am now experiencing uncontrolled flashbacks, body memories, nausea, vomiting, panic attacks and anxiety." He replied, "I see the Paxil isn't working," I told him, "Sandy recommended me getting a referral to a psychiatrist and that is why I am here."

He told me to get on the exam table as he checked my breathing. Then he sat in his chair as he explained the new medicine and said, "The receptionist will schedule an appointment with a psychiatrist." Then I told him, "When I switched my primary physician to you, I was impressed right away. On my first visit you took the time to gather routine family background information. You asked about family history, including mental illness bi-polar, PTSD, etc. I felt very comfortable to be completely honest with you. We agreed that day to wait on the medication to see if I could do it alone with exercise and diet. You reviewed all the tests that were done in the past and recently then asked me if I was depressed. I said, No because I was used to feeling that way, it was normal to me. Now, that I am in therapy. I am learning about what post-traumatic stress disorder is and starting to learn what my body needs when things trigger me and how to cope. I experience body memories like each day I am being raped and emotionally abused. I just want to say "Thank You" for treating me with respect, taking extra time with me, and talking me into getting the counseling I needed. Over the years a lot of doctors were unkind to me because they thought I was making up my symptoms because they couldn't find anything wrong with me. I wish that would be part of physician training to take a class on mental illness." Dr. Anderson cleared his throat and said, "I appreciate that." I could tell he doesn't get many compliments.

He finished our visit by telling me to take the paperwork to the receptionist and she will handle making the appointment. He held the door open as I walked through it he said, "You take care of yourself." I felt there was hope that I would be back on track.

I gave the receptionist the paperwork with my head down because the "child within" felt ashamed for needing help. She looked at the doctor's orders and consulted with another person, as she pointed to me. They were whispering but I heard the words STAT and crisis care.

I watched the other receptionist as she got on the phone. Then I heard, "This is Jane, from Dr. Anderson's office." "He has a patient that is in crisis and needs an appointment immediately! He doesn't have any openings! This patient is in crisis care with PTSD "uncontrolled," the patient needs to be seen immediately today," with authority in her voice.

The "child within" started to panic as I called my boss, Jenny. She answered the phone and I told her, "I can't return to work today because my blood pressure is too high 142/118!" She asked, "Who is this?" I told her, "It is Leslie." She replied, "Oh, okay." I explained, "My doctor also wants me to see a psychiatrist right away today!" I began to cry as I leaned against the wall resting my head on my forearm. Then I became hysterical telling my boss, "I am terrified about being admitted to a locked unit." I paused for a moment to catch my breath. I continued, "I can't be admitted because my family depends on me to feed and to take care of them!" I explained, "I have no more time to take off work because I have depleted my PTO hours with counseling and doctor appointments. I am also worried about keeping my job."

Jenny reassured me with a soft, comforting and calming voice. She said, "I will do everything I can to help your family but the most important thing is for you to take care of yourself." She reassured me, "She'll work out the PTO hours with the Human Resources Department and that you don't have to worry about job security because we couldn't get along without you."

While still on the phone with my boss, a nurse returned to my side, guiding me back to an exam room with compassion as she wrapped her arm around my shoulder to turn me then had her hand on the mid section of my back as she slowly led me. She said with a gentle voice, "It is okay, Leslie, we are going to get you some help." I told Jenny, "I have to hang up but I promise to call you when I receive more information."

I sat in the exam room while trying to contact my husband, Ramone, which failed. Then I attempted to call my dad but that failed too. Dr. Anderson returned and calmly sat down slowly in the chair with his hand folded on his lap. "Leslie I think it is time you go to the hospital for an evaluation."

The "child within" surfaced, as I tried to stop crying and straighten myself up, by trying to act and be normal. I asked, "Why?" He replied because "You're freaking out on the staff and they are scared!" I explained, "I am crying because I am scared of the unknown. I have never been though something like this before. The receptionists' frightened me because they were making urgent calls to the psychiatrist in front of me. They panicked, so I became panicked." I reassured him that I didn't yell at anyone or behave inappropriately. The "child within" felt he was punishing her for being a bad girl. He replied, "I will talk to my staff because I didn't know they did that."

He said, "What do you want to do?" I replied, "I want to wait for the psychiatrist appointment." He asked, "Are you suicidal?" I replied, "No!" He agreed to let me go to my mother's house and he would call me in an hour to let me know what will happen.

As we both got up, he opened the door for me. As I walked down the hallway to the lobby, he said, "I will call you in an hour" and he repeated, "You take care of yourself." I quickly bypassed the lobby as I rushed out the door, without looking at the staff.

When I reached my van, I was worried about driving because I was really dizzy. I tried to call Ramone one more time. Then I called my mom to see if my dad returned home and he didn't. I told her, "I will just drive myself." She was concerned but I told her it is only minutes away.

I took a deep breath while my hands were shaking as I turned the van on. I prayed to God to keep me and the other people on the street safe. I got as far as McDonalds, which was about a ¼ mile into town. I stopped and went through the drive thru. Then I continued a few more blocks to my mother's house. As I pulled into the driveway, I felt a sigh of relief.

When I entered the kitchen door, my mom was nervously waiting for me. When she saw me, she jumped up and rushed toward me saying, "Thank God you made it," as she gave me a tight hug. I sat down and told her I felt dizzy and sick.

My mom asked, "What are they doing for you?" I explained the plan and she agreed I should be in the hospital. I started to cry and panic again because the "child within" was scared to go to the hospital. I told my mom, "I don't want to be trapped on a locked unit." She said, "Oh honey but you need to go so you can get help. I love you honey. I am so sorry this is happening to you."

I said, "I have to eat I feel faint. I didn't eat or sleep last night. I also didn't eat yet this morning." I told her the doctor would call in an hour. She agreed I needed to eat and then sleep. She would wait for the phone call.

I slowly shuffled to my mother's bedroom as I tried to keep my balance because the dizziness was overwhelming. I crawled into her bed and covered myself with her soft and fluffy comforters. I felt safe and loved in my mommy's bed. Then without warning, I started to cry as the flashbacks returned as I relived the rape when I was 14 years old. The visuals, feelings, and the guilt, of me not reporting it to save the other girls surfaced. I was sobbing hysterically as I tried to muffle the sounds in my mommy's pillows I screamed, "You had no right to rape me and the other girls! Bret Hanks is a rapist." "Finally, after 21 years of holding it in, I said it out loud."

My mother quickly ran into the room. "Are you okay honey?" as she hugged me. My tears blurred my vision. Covered in tears seemed to help me to tell my mom what happened to me. My mom felt so bad, guilty, and was crying. "I am so sorry I thought he was a good boy!" "I never thought he would do this." I felt the need to comfort my mom by telling her, "It's okay mom. I know now by talking to you these past days that you were dealing with your own abuse. You were probably at the same place I am now when I was little. I know we will get through this together." I felt lucky to have my mother's help now and it meant a lot to me that she was willing to go through the healing process with me. I told my mom I needed to rest and she said, "Okay" as she dried her tears and walked away.

Shortly I heard the phone ring and my mom yelled "Leslie it is for you." I quickly got to the phone "Hi Leslie, this is Dr. Anderson." "We were unable to get a psychiatrist appointment because they are closed to new patients. We have two options: (1) "I could try to put you on medications until you see a psychiatrist. or (2) "You go in as Crisis Care to the emergency room so the psychiatrist on call can evaluate you. He can prescribe the medicine you need right now."

"What do you suggest?" He answered, "I suggest you go into the emergency room as a patient in need of crisis care." I started to panic when I asked, "What do I say to them?" He replied, "Be honest with them that your PTSD symptoms are out of control!" I agreed with him, "I will do what you say because I respect and trust your judgment."

I started to panic and my heart was beating fast I felt it was urgent that I call my therapist to tell her what was happening. As Sandy answered the phone, I heard her calming and comforting voice. She asked, "What is going on, honey?" I was hysterically while trying to explain, "They are going to put me on a locked unit!" Sandy told me, "Calm down and breathe in and out slowly." I continued, "This makes me feel like I will be trapped and unable to leave." Dr. Anderson told me to go to the Emergency Room in Crisis Care for my PTSD." Sandy asked, "Are you suicidal?" I replied, "No!" She reassured, "They wouldn't lock you on that unit because that unit is only for suicidal people. They most likely will give you a regular hospital bed and you will be free to go at anytime."

I called my boss and started to sob as I told her, "I am being admitted to the hospital to see a psychiatrist and to get on immediate medications to help me with my PTSD symptoms. I am so sorry I can't come to work for awhile." She responded with her soft and comforting voice. "I am so proud of you for getting the help. It is important to take care of Leslie." I responded, "Please authorize a negative PTO balance because my financial situation is bad." "I need my whole check to feed my family." She reassured me that she would take care of my family while I was in the hospital. I felt relieved that I could focus on myself without worrying about my family.

When I hung up the phone with Jenny, I knew it was time to do the hardest thing, admitting I needed help. Stuffing memories and emotions was no longer working. The need for medication was evident from all the anxiety, depression, crying spells, self sabotage, and angry outbursts that surfaced when my family triggered me, unknown to them.

As my husband walked in, I apologized for him worrying about me but I said, "It is time to admit me into the hospital." His face seemed sad for me but he quickly sprung into action as he helped me down the stairs and out the back door. My parents were crying telling me everything was going to be okay.

My son, 4 years old, walked in front of us. I tried to talk to him as I was crying really hard while explaining, "Mommy has to go to the hospital for a while." He had an angry look on his face as he crossed his arms and his lip was curled outward. In a tiny sad voice, "I don't want you to go mommy." I told him, "I have to," as I asked for a hug. He said, "No, I don't want a hug. I don't want you to go." My heart broke as I got into the van and Ramone put Kota in his seat. Kota didn't talk the whole way to the hospital. I felt overwhelmed with sadness because I knew I was affecting him emotionally by crying.

Flashbacks in Post-Traumatic Stress Disorder: Surviving the Flood

Entering Crisis Care

As we reached the ER, I walked in by myself as Ramone parked the van. I reached the receptionist desk and was crying hysterically, my body jerking in response. The receptionist asked "Can I help you?" with a concerned look and caution, as she slowly approached me and helped me sit in the chair beside her.

She repeated, "What can I do for you?" I tried to explain in between crying and sobbing, "I need crisis care and need to be admitted." "My post-traumatic stress disorder is out of control and I can't cope any longer." I continued to explain, "The flashbacks and body memories are too much to bear." She asked a few questions to verify who I was, my insurance, and then had me sit in the lobby, as she called the nurse to come and assist her.

I sat there and tried to reach for Kota to try to calm him but he didn't want me to touch him because he was scared of me. My husband, Ramone, comforted him and told him, "Mommy will be okay." "She just has a booboo and the doctors will fix what is wrong and mommy will be home soon."

I tried to calm myself by closing my eyes to lessen my son's terror but, I jumped and went into a fight or flight mode as I heard the door open loudly and a nurse appeared. She gently said, "Are you Leslie?" She placed her hand softly on my back while explaining, "We will help you feel better." I jumped again as the nurse pressed the handicap button to open the door with a loud noise but my reaction didn't seem as terrifying.

She walked me down the hallway to a room. I sat down in a chair as I started to cry really hard again. My tears blocked my vision and helped me to tell the nurse, "I was raped at the age of 14 and the flashbacks and body memories are too much to handle while seeing it in my mind."

She tried to comfort me while another person came to take my blood pressure and this time it was 160/118. I explained, "I saw my physician earlier today and he ordered another blood pressure medication but I haven't picked it up yet because I am here." The nurse asked for the list of medications I was on but I was unable to tell her. I kept repeating to call the pharmacy they will tell you.

The ER physician came in and sat down on the rolling stool in front of me. He asked, "What is wrong today?" "Is it depression?" I replied, "Yes, but it is also my PTSD, flashbacks, body memories and anxiety." "I just can't handle stuffing my emotions anymore!" "I need to heal. I was so strong for 32 years."

I explained each individual trauma in my life and after each one he confirmed, "You are not being hurt presently at home are you? You feel safe at home, right?" I explained, "The feelings of being unsafe are due to the past traumas."

He told me in a compassionate voice "Leslie those traumas and rape are in the past." "You are not being hurt anymore." I replied, "My intelligence knows it happened in the past, but the flashbacks and body memories make me experience it in the present. Every time a flashback surfaces it is like being raped over and over again." He seemed to understand as he said, "Let me work on getting you admitted."

The nurse returned, "I got the information from your pharmacy." As she saw my distress, anxiety and that my crying was increasing, she said, "Leslie would you like me to give you something to help you relax so you can get some relief?" I pleaded, "Yes, please help me!" She told me it had to be given in the butt. I agreed it was okay.

Shortly later, I felt relaxed, tired but still dizzy. The doctor came in and updated me that they do have a room but it will take some time to turn the room over. On his way out I asked, "Please shut the light off so I can rest. Also, please remind my husband in the waiting room to pick up our daughters from school."

Some time passed and from a distance, I heard my husband's voice and a nurse. I heard the nurse say; "I know we put her in one of these rooms." The nurse announced loudly, "Here she is as she turned on the bright light." As my eyes tried to adjust to the light, I asked about the children, especially Kota. Ramone said, "I took all the children to Victoria's house so I can be with you." I explained what happened as my body still was jerking and I was sobbing. He comforted me and said, "Everything will be all right." He reassured me he wasn't going to leave me.

Then the security guard strolled in with a wheelchair and said, "I am your escort upstairs to your room." He wheeled me to the elevator and pressed the third floor. I had a sinking feeling in my stomach as I looked at Ramone. As the elevator door opened we went around the corner, I saw in big letters "Behavioral Health." I became upset as I watched the security guard put his keys in to the key hole to gain access to the unit. I yelled, "I knew I was going to be trapped and locked in!" My anxiety and panic surfaced again as we entered the unit. I glanced behind me and saw the doors slam shut as my freedom was taken away.

I arrived at my room and the nurses came in to check all my belongings. I felt like I was in a prison. I asked the nurse "Why am I on this unit?" "I am not suicidal!" She said, "Maybe this was the only bed open." She reassured me I was in good hands. They also gave me medication.

Shortly after, the nurse returned with most of my belongings, except for my Pepsi and spiral notebook. They didn't allow caffeine because it's considered a stimulant and the wire on the notebook could be used to cut myself.

I repeated angrily, "I am not suicidal!" I felt all the control of my choices were being taken away, just like when I was abused and raped. My husband calmly said, "I will bring a different notebook without a spiral and I'll get decaffeinated Pepsi for you when I come to visit.

A few minutes later, the nurse told Ramone that visiting hours are not until 6:00 p.m. and that he had to leave so I could get some rest. I pleaded with her to let him stay because I was terrified to be locked inside with all the crazy people. I heard a man in the hallway screaming and talking nonsense while security arrived to assist the nurses.

I held my husband's hand tightly and refused to let go. I pleaded with him, "Please stay, I am so frightened." I explained frantically to the nurse, "We have never been apart." His face was full of compassion and love with tears in his eyes he separated my hand from his. He promised to visit later. I stood outside my door as I watched the nurse buzz him out. He blew me a kiss and said, "I will be back later," as the door slammed shut. I was locked in unable to escape.

Chapter 14
Being Honest With Myself

Day 1, Thursday, May 12, 2011- Visiting Hours

I was lying in my bed motionless staring out the window waiting for Ramone to return. I had horrible thoughts racing through my mind. Maybe he wouldn't return and I would be trapped in here forever.

I felt so tired because of all the pills I was on. I felt dizzy, numb, and like I had no emotions. After supper came and gone then it was visiting hours. My boss came to visit me. I was comforted by her quiet, gentle voice as she reminded me that, "She would help in any way she could." She reassured me of my job security and that Emma, Joan and she was praying for me along with all the coworkers and the members of my church. She gave me a hug and said, "I will visit again tomorrow and ordered me to get some rest."

I was startled as I heard a knock at the door. It was Ramone. He returned for me! He sat down in the chair next to my bed as I reached for his hand and held it tighter than before. He stood up and gave me a loving kiss and a tight embrace. He was trying to draw out the humorous side of me while he commented on my hair. He asked, "Are you trying a new hair style? Maybe a Mohawk?" He made me feel normal because he didn't treat me any different than he would if we were at home. The visiting hours went by fast. I knew I had to say good-bye again but this time it wasn't as hard because I knew he would return.

I took a shower to relax and then lay down on my bed. Then the flashbacks started again: the set up of the room, when I was raped, the smell of sperm, and pain in my vaginal area started. I was crying so hard the nurse heard me. She came in and asked, "What is happening in here?" I told her what I was experiencing. She helped me out of my bed and with a gentle hand on my back guided me to the nurses' station for my sleeping pills. After I returned to my room, I climbed into bed in the fetal position and fell asleep.

Day 2, Friday, May 13, 2011
The Psychiatrist came in to talk to me. He asked, "What is happening with you?" I explained about my anxiety, depression, flashbacks and body memories. I also explained about Dr. Anderson telling me to admit myself for crisis care because there was no psychiatrist open to new patients. I also told him I was in therapy with Sandy.

He had read my records. He told me that on top of PTSD that I also had bi-polar. I didn't agree because my sister was bi-polar. When she gets sick, she is out of her mind and each ego-state is shown outward as multiple personalities. I have never experienced those behaviors. He explained there were different levels of bi-polar and my sister's was a lot more serious. "You have a chemical imbalance in your brain and the pills I am prescribing will balance it out." He would double my dose of sleeping pills because I couldn't sleep because of the body memories.

I called Sandy right away and explained that the psychiatrist said, "I am bi-polar but I didn't agree. My anxiety, ups and downs were due to trauma and flashbacks. I need a second opinion because how can someone talk to me for less than five minutes and diagnose me with bipolar?" Sandy said, "I agreed. You can get a second opinion after you get out of the hospital and find a permanent psychiatrist."

Shortly after hanging up with Sandy, there was a knock at my door. It was Sue the "Coping Skills" teacher. She softly said, "You need to come to Coping Skills group because it is a mandatory group that the doctor ordered for you." When I walked into the room, I saw three other people sitting at the table.

I timidly took my seat as Sue explained the "Wellness Wheel". The hardest thing for me was to fill it out honestly and to stop pretending everything was fine when it wasn't. I felt I was still okay with the: intellectual, spiritual, psychological, and environmental functioning. There were three trouble areas: emotional, physical and social. These items made the wheel unable to spin. Then I had to answer the questions:

Which dimensions of life are you most well? Intellectual- knowing I need help and seeking it. Spiritual—surrendering to God for healing and help. Psychological—adaptive ability to troubleshoot.

In which are you least well? Emotional—PTSD symptoms are out of control. Bi-polar? Physical—I am obese. I have a feeling of failure because I gained so much weight. Social- in-between belonging and alone. Alone at home because anxiety/triggers, disrespect from the kids. Belonging at work because I receive respect and my employer and coworkers depend on me. Vocational-in-between satisfied and dissatisfied. I need a title change from Secretary to Office Manager along with a raise to match the title. I am doing the job but not being compensated for it.

How do you feel about what you see? Sad, because usually I have everything in control and now everything is out of my control. I feel like I failed myself and my family.

How well do the patterns you see correspond to what you expect to see? Not surprised at the good because I still have control in those areas. I'm also not surprised that my wheel is lopsided because I am sick with PTSD symptoms of flashbacks, body memories, anxiety and depression.

What improvements would you like to see in your wheel profile? Social increased—I need medication, guidance, and God's grace, family and prayer support to heal. Physical restored—focus on myself while making healthy food choices. Analyze why I am eating when I go to the cupboard or refrigerator. Is it because I am hungry or do I need to comfort the "child within?" Emotional—emotions stabilize: controlling of triggers, coping in healthy ways, and managing stress healthily too.

List two or three ways that can immediately round out your wheel and make these improvements. Physical—exercise, lose weight, portion control, and decrease/ eliminate soda. Social—reconnect with family and friends and do activities to enjoy living life to its fullest potential. Emotional—being in control without emotionally breaking down. Have a feeling of strength and happiness, "a survivor." Managing triggers, anxiety, and depression will help accomplish these emotional needs. Vocational—work with Jenny to change my job title and wage to reflect what I am actually doing.

After each member of the group shared, the class ended and everyone went to lunch. After lunch, we had another group called "Task Skills." At this class we could express ourselves through all kinds of art. The cabinets were full of supplies and different art projects. I decided for my first project to pick something easy, which was to color a velvet bag. I was so drugged from that pills that I was afraid of messing up my project.

I felt free to do whatever I wanted. If I wanted to color my bee pink and blue I could. I was one that didn't want to blend in. I like to stick out a little. The "child within" really enjoyed playing because she was always trying to survive, not playing.

Before supper, Father Mark came to perform the anointing of the sick. He spent time to listen about the abuse, neglect, and the rape I experienced. He responded with compassion and assured me of God's love for me. He then blessed me with holy oil on my hands and forehead. We

Flashbacks in Post-Traumatic Stress Disorder: Surviving the Flood

prayed to Saint Dympna for healing of mental affliction. After Father blessed me, I told him I felt great strength, comfort and thanked him for coming.

My boss came back to visit me. I told her Father Mark came and anointed me. She was happy that I was doing better. I updated her about my medications. I also shared some of the trauma I went through. I thanked her for checking on my family. She reassured me they had enough food and were doing fine. We also talked about work and that everything is fine. She told me my coworker, Emma, would be in tomorrow to visit me.

She told me all the coworkers and my parish was praying for me. Also, Joan called, while on a business trip, and Jenny updated her about me. She was very worried. She asked Jenny to tell me she was sending special prayers for me. I felt lucky to have a support system of many people praying for God's grace and healing for me. Jenny gave me a hug and said she would visit again.

My sisters, Andie and Sonya, called to check on me. I told them how I felt overly medicated. They both had been through the same process and reassured me I would feel better as I became used to the medications. I said, "I hope it happens soon because I am sick of the dizziness. When I walk, I feel drunk like I could trip or fall." They both offered me love and compassion as they promised to call me again.

Ramone was the next visitor. He followed through with buying me snacks and a non-spiral notebook and caffeine-free Pepsi. I could relax because my needs were taken care of.

I felt an overwhelming need to talk to Ramone about the details of the rape so he could understand what happened to me. It was my way of explaining why for the past 6 years, sex was so hard because of body memories, smells of sperm, and the fear of seeing my rapist's face in his face, while having sex.

I was crying and holding his hand asking if he loved me. I was scared he wouldn't want me for his wife anymore. I felt soiled, no good, and worthless. He replied, "Of course I love you." He reassured me he wasn't going anywhere. I expressed the need to report the rape to the police. I knew they couldn't do anything about it for me. But it would be in the records, if Bret rapes again. My husband said, "I will support you in anything you feel you need to do but first take care of yourself."

After visiting hours ended, I couldn't stop my anxiety and the crying continued. The nurse, Laura, could hear me from the hallway, as she passed my room. She came in and shut the door half way so there was privacy. She took a seat beside my bed and asked, "Honey, what is wrong?" She held out her hand and I accepted it while she slowly rubbed it with compassion in her eyes. I felt safe enough to explain to her about the rape, abuse, and neglect. She reassured me that I would get through this rough time because she could tell I was strong and a survivor. She gently helped me out of bed, as she half hugged me. She replied, "I am so sorry all this happened to you." She slowly walked me to the nurses' station to get my Depokote and my sleeping pills.

I took a shower and then went to bed. I had an okay sleep but still had body memories of me being choked over and over again. I kept coughing, waking up and drinking water throughout the night.

Day 3, Saturday, May 14, 2011
I woke up in the morning as a male nurse said, "Good morning, did you have a nice sleep?" I replied, "Not really", as I look around in a daze. Then he made the comment that while I was asleep he took my vitals. He checked on me throughout the night to make sure I was okay. As he left the room, my mind began to wonder and asked the question: If I was that

much out of it, did he touch me or have sex with me while I was asleep? I trusted my body because I didn't feel violated. I determined it was just fear and anxiety again.

A few minutes later, the psychiatrist arrived. He asked, "How are you doing?" I told him of the flashbacks, body memories and smell of sperm that made me upset. I also told him I feel dizzy, numb and unsteady. He told me it would be that way until my body gets used to the medication. He said, "You'll have good and bad days. You need to let go of the bad memories to be able to live normally."

After the psychiatrist left, I was upset and disappointed when a nurse came in and announced that Task Skills group was cancelled. The teacher sprained her ankle. I wanted to express myself through art. I went back to sleep, and then woke up in time for lunch.

Visiting hours finally came and to my surprise my parents brought my daughters to see me. My daughters came up to my bed and immediately hugged me really tight saying, "We love you mommy." I started to cry and said, "I am so sorry for being overly protective." They replied, "It is okay mom that is what a good mom does so the children don't get hurt."

My girls took Kota to find a puzzle and to keep him busy while my parents and I talked. My mom and dad told me I was a great mother. I updated them on my medications and diagnosis. I started to cry as I said, "Mom, the rape is haunting me." Just before I was admitted, I told her in detail what happened to me. I explained how good it felt to be able to talk to her about what happened because it was killing me by holding it in for 21 years. She told me not to worry about her because she felt sad for her little girl. She said, "When your kids hurt, the mother hurts too." She started to cry and told me about her traumas, as a small girl. I didn't know this about my mom. I hugged her and told her I was sorry it happened to her too.

She explained the reason she didn't come to see me right away was because it was too hard for her to see me on this unit. It brought back memories for her when she was on the same unit five times for alcohol abuse. I was there each time holding her hand through it all. Throughout our conversation, my dad sat on the chair hunched over his cane and would say something encouraging every so often.

I told my parents that I have forgiven them because they no longer denied my memories. Instead, they were apologizing to me, crying with me and hugging me. I finally felt loved and comforted by my parents and the "child within" felt that her needs for emotional stability were being met. I finally realized that they didn't have the tools to be better parents because my dad had PTSD from the Vietnam War and my mom was recovering from alcoholism and from her own trauma.

I finally felt I could leave the memories of neglect, injury, and no parental guidance behind me. I would never forget how I felt or what happened and how it has affected me. I now had a better way of coping by remembering my parents were struggling as I am now.

My children returned and my youngest daughter, Veronica, who was 13 years old and 5'8 tall said, "A lady asked me if Kota was my son! Do I look that old?" Kota said with his hands on his hips, "And I told that lady that she was my sister, not my mom!" We all laughed because Kota set that lady straight.

My oldest daughter, Sabrina, age 15, looked like the cat that swallowed the mouse. She said, "Mommy do you want to hear some good news?" I said, "Of course, we love good news!" She had her arms and hands together, while swaying with a big grin on her face. "I got my period today." My mother said, "Sabrina that is wonderful!" Sabrina said, "I wanted you to be the first to know because you are my mom." She went on to explain, "I didn't tell Aunt Victoria, Grandpa, Grandma, dad or even my sister. Veronica said, "Heah, sisters tell each other everything." I hugged Sabrina and started to cry because it meant so much to me that she came to me first. My dad was looking weak, as my mother, Rita, said, "It is time to go say good bye to your mother."

I rested for a few hours, and then I looked up and see a friendly face. It was Emma from work. She told me everything was going well at work, as they prepared for the rummage sale. We talked about some of my challenges with trauma and the guilt I felt for not reporting the rape. I told her what I was learning about taking care of myself in group and the importance to set goals and action plans on how to help myself live with my PTSD.

I shared one of my action plan items, which was to report the rape to the police, once I left the hospital. She emphasized the importance of healing, taking care of only me and not anyone else. She was concerned of a relapse. I told her I was journaling each day and joked that I wasn't sure if it made any sense because of how drugged and dizzy I felt. "The force was guiding my pen and will help me write," I told her. "Someday I hope to be a published writer to help give women or men like me hope and strength when they read it." She gave me a hug and told me she had to go work at the animal shelter but told me to keep doing what I am doing and to remember, "You are strong, the strongest person I know."

When visiting hours were over, the nurse announced that it was movie time. I went and sat down in the lobby with other patients and one family member. The daughter of a patient asked, "What's the movie you're going to see?" I said, "Well considering where we are, I don't think there will be any action or violence so it will probably be a Disney animated cartoon movie, perhaps Dumbo the elephant." She replied, "I hope not." I replied, "We'll see." I felt myself smiling ear to ear. The humorous Leslie was coming back. It made me happy because my sisters always told me I could be a comedian because I was good at making people laugh.

Shortly the nurse came in to set up the DVD player, as a patient glanced at me and said, "What's the movie tonight?" She replied it is, "Up!" He asked, "What is that?" The nurse replied, "It is a Disney animated cartoon. It is really good. I really liked it." The nurse left to get popcorn and soda. I glanced at the daughter of the patient and started to laugh. I said, "At least it's not Dumbo the elephant cartoon. Did I call it or what?" All the patients were laughing. "You sure did!"

Chapter 15
Trusting Myself

Day 4- Sunday, May 15, 2011

At breakfast, I was pulled out to see the psychiatrist. I told him of my symptoms, and I was still feeling drugged and unsteady. He told me again it would take some time to adjust to the medicine. I told him of the caffeine withdrawal I was experiencing. He agreed to allow one caffeine soda a day. He also lowered the dosage on my sleeping pills. After I was done talking to the psychiatrist, I went back to finish my breakfast.

After breakfast the nurse announced that we would have the Task Skills group that was cancelled the day before. I was as happy as I quickly jumped out of my bed and went to the room before the rest of the group arrived.

We were told to pick out a project so I chose a wooden butterfly and colored it. When I was finished I asked, "Do we have time for another project?" The teacher answered, "Yes!" I decided to draw a picture of my safe place with a tree, sun, and waterfall with rocks at the base. I imagined myself dipping my feet in the water and touching the bottom with the soft rocks in the cool and soothing waters. I felt calm and happy. My safe place is an actual place in upstate New York. My sister, Andie, took me there to share her special place and to write poetry. Also, on the bottom of the picture was my "child within" on the left with the statements, "I am starting to trust my adult self to take care of me." "I am starting to feel loved and safe" "I don't need to surface as much."

On the right side is a drawing of my adult self with the statements, "Work too hard for everyone. I have to be the mom to my "child within".

She needs my love and protection." "There were flashes of feelings of being successful in my job and deserving of praise from my boss." "When I received praise from my boss it is hard to accept it or believe it." After I completed the picture the teacher laminated it so it would be protected.

We still had time left so I did another project. I drew a picture of a bird and took feathers of all colors and pasted them on the paper. On top are two flowers and on the bottom were two stripes of purple fabric. I am so drugged the "child within" surfaced and started petting the feathers. I felt silly and playful as I comment on how soft the feathers are as I held it up to my face saying "They are so soft and they feel safe and calming as I giggled like a little girl." The teacher took my picture and cut the empty scrapbook cover and helped me to paste my picture on the cover. She said, "This is the start of your scrapbook for your artwork." The goal for tomorrow would be to create a picture for the back cover.

After I got back to my room, I remembered a patient was going home today. He explained in group his goal was to lose weight and to eat healthy. I told him about the *Glycemic Index* cookbook. He seemed excited to try it, as he wrote down the name of the book. I called Ramone to see if I still had an extra copy of the cookbook. Everyone in my family received the cookbook for Christmas last year. I asked Ramone to bring the extra copy to visiting hours.

My first visitor was my sister, Victoria. I was surprised and happy as I saw her walk through the door. She sat down by me and asked, "How are you doing today?" I told her about my depression and anxiety. I said, "I still feel out of control with my emotions." I told her the experience is now flipped, because she came in here about three times for suicide attempts and mom came in for alcohol abuse several times. I apologized to Victoria because at that time I believed she could control her feelings and the attempts on her life were her needing attention. I started to cry as I said, "I am so sorry. I didn't know. I now know how you must have felt."

She replied, "It's okay. You didn't know about mental illness but now you're experiencing it. There is no need to apologize. I love you and want you to get better." I felt better knowing one more item I felt guilty about was resolved and forgiven.

My next visitor was my boss, Jenny. I felt bad because my anxiety, panic, and depression were at a high level. I talked about my trauma and how it affected me. She asked, "Do you get triggered at the office?" I said, "Yes, zoning out, vomiting and panic attacks, but I was able to use coping skills to get through it quickly. It was usually something that triggered me by my thoughts, not my environment."

I told her about the paperwork I received from our Human Resources Department that upset me. For FMLA it stated that I had to use PTO hours to get paid. I currently didn't have PTO hours because I used them for all the therapy appointments for my daughters and myself. This meant I wouldn't get a paycheck but worse my health insurance could be cancelled along with other benefits, if I was unable to pay them. I asked her to please authorize a negative PTO balance so I could get my full paycheck to support my family and pay my health insurance. I explained to her I couldn't afford to be more in debt with medical bills and confessed I was already $20,000 in debt. She assured me that she would do anything to help me. She assured me she wouldn't let the HR Director discontinue my health insurance. She promised to call the Human Resources Department in the morning to make special arrangements for me.

I told her, "Thank you, because I was going to try to fool the doctors so I could get out sooner if I was going to lose my income and benefits." She told me to stay and get the help I needed so I can get well again. She reassured me that the office was fine but they didn't want to lose me as an employee. I felt so comforted by how loving and supportive she was of me. I never knew of an employer who actually cared for their employees the way she did. I received a phone call and it was my other sister, Sonya, calling from New York. Jenny whispered, "I will let you talk to your family." She gave me a hug and assured me of her prayers.

I returned to the phone and gave my sister, Sonya, a short update on my progress along with my challenges that I was literally facing. She told me of her experience of losing control. Each of us has gone through similar situations but I was the youngest and the last one to go through the process. She assured me that everything will get better as I go through therapy and admitted she was in therapy for years. She said she loved me and would call again.

Then a few minutes later my other sister, Andie, also from New York called. I gave her an identical update and challenges. Her words were comforting. She told me that in the future I would be able to control my emotions instead of them controlling me. I would be able to live a better life with my family. I will be known as a SURIVOR. I felt a feeling of empowerment come over me as she said I would be a SURIVOR. I always knew she was a survivor but never saw myself as one. It meant a lot for her to tell me that. She told me to keep up the good work and she would call me tomorrow.

Next my husband peeked in my room and in came the kids. He brought the extra cookbook. I went into the dining room and set the book next to one of the patients. His eyes looked surprised and he thanked me for a nice gift. I told him, "It is my contribution to your healing process." I wished him good luck because it was his day to leave the hospital. I went to my seat and quickly ate so I could return to my room to visit with my family.

I was so happy to see them. Kota, my four year old was getting antsy but I knew what to do to entertain him. I said, "Come here, Kota. Do you want to know a secret" as he came near me to listen carefully. I asked, "Do you want a treat?" He got excited as he replied "Yes" and asked, "Where and what do you have?" I pulled the drawer out beside me and took out the trail mix with the M&M's and then closed the drawer. Then Kota forcefully reopened the drawer and said, "What else do you have in here?" as he looked he saw garlic crackers and gummy bears. He chose the gummy bears. Kota glanced at me with his young boy's eyes and said, "You can share. You don't need these." My daughters were happy saying we didn't know you had treats!" I said, "I'm willing to share but leave some for me please." My teenage daughters love treats and they are growing girls and seem to be hungry most of the time. Shortly after snack time, visiting hours were over. My family gave me hugs and kisses and said good-bye. I think knowing I wasn't free to leave made me feel trapped, like I did when my trauma was happening. I finished my evening with a nice hot shower, watched TV, as I was journaling my inpatient experience.

Day 5—Monday, May 16, 2011

I was just finishing breakfast when the psychiatrist waved for me to come back to my room to meet with him. He asked, "How was your sleep?" I told him I was really out. I told him, "I thought you were going to change my dosage on the sleeping pills!" He said, "Yeah, I was but still think you need the 100 mg pill to sleep." I pleaded with him, "Please reduce it because in the morning I feel drugged and the nurses give me four more pills, and two more in the evening." He said he would change it but I wasn't confident because he didn't follow through the night before. I reported, "I had no flashbacks or body memories last night." He was pleased and said, "Maybe you can go home on Tuesday."

Then I went to Coping Skills group. We worked on how to identify problem areas, set goals, and create action steps on how to accomplish those goals, identify what is stopping us from achieving our goals and what the staff can do to help us while in the hospital.

Problem Areas: 1. Flashbacks of rape and body memories. 2. Anxiety, panic, depression and a feeling of being trapped. 3. Need to be in control all the time in order to feel safe. 4. Overly protective of my children. 5. Financial issues.

I chose the two following priorities to concentrate on: **Priority #1**—Flashbacks of rape and body memories. **Goal:** When the flashbacks or body memories surface, I feel like the rape is happening in the present and the feelings are overwhelming. I would like to find ways to control my anxiety, panic, depression by being in control instead of being emotionally out of control. **Action Steps**: 1. I feel the need to release the guilt of not reporting the rape to the police by reporting it now. 2. I will try relaxing, positive imagery, and deep breathing to get my mind off of it. 3. I will start exercising to get the endorphins going to balance my moods.

What's stopping you for achieving your goal? I am scared. I feel the responsibility for all the rapes Bret did after mine. I know he did this to many girls based on what he did after he was finished. I need to report the rape to resolve the guilt I have carried with me for 21 years, so it will be on record in case another victim comes forward. I know it is probably too late for justice for me but hopefully not for the next victim.

How can staff help? When I have an episode they can comfort me and reassure me I am safe. Help me to visualize my safe place that I drew.

Priority #2—Anxiety, panic, depression and feeling of being trapped. **Goal:** I would like to be in control of my emotions so the triggers at home don't affect me to the extent of yelling at my children. My children need to respect my boundaries and they are constantly testing me and it is difficult when it triggers me back to my trauma. **Action Plans:** 1. When I notice the triggers, I will be honest with my family about how I am feeling. 2. Remove myself from the area or away from the person triggering me. 3. Go for a walk to calm myself down.

How can staff help? I don't have many triggers in the hospital when it comes to people. If my kids come and it gets overwhelming or I am sad after they leave, the staff can comfort me.

What's stopping you from achieving your goal? I was keeping what was happening to me a secret so my family was in the dark about my condition until I was admitted to the hospital. Even my husband didn't know the extent of what was going on with me. My panic attacks started 11 years ago when my husband and I first met. I was able to hide my struggles until now at the age of 35. I felt depressed and emotionally overwhelmed most of the time and little things bothered me to the extreme. I was always stressed in the flight or fight mode waiting to protect myself from a threat that wasn't there. I also felt too fat and like it was too late for me to get healthy. It was easier to give up.

Then the teacher, Sue, asked us to list five personal strengths we have. This was very hard for me. ***My personal strengths are:*** 1. I am empathic to people. 2. I am humorous and can make people laugh even in difficult times, me included. 3. I am very organized and proactive. 4. I can function at a high level even though I wasn't feeling well. 5. I am friendly, outgoing, and helpful and enjoy helping coworkers and guests. We finished the coping class by sharing with the group our first plan of action that we would carry out once we left the hospital.

I went back to my room and expected to take a nap before going to Task Skills group. I was greeted with a gift. The nurse, Laura, came in and said, "Father Ted came when you were in-group and we don't interrupt you while you are in-group." I felt disappointed but was anxious to see what was inside the box. Laura stayed while I opened the box and lifted the contents out. I was in awe of what was inside: A beautiful bouquet of plastic flowers with a glass vase of different colors of purple, green yellow. The vase was wide with curvy ends on top. It was so breath taking but because it was glass, Laura had to take it away from me right away and replace it with a plastic vase until I left the hospital. I showed Laura the card that made me laugh it said, "Thinking of you. Enjoy the flowers, no watering needed!" With a happy face! I said, "Laura this is a private joke at work because I either underwater the plants or overwater them." "I feel like they are consistently close to death." I was so happy I rested awhile before going to another group.

On the way to Task Skills group, I saw a former coworker, Tiffany, from my previous job. She was doing an assessment for a possible patient admission to the nursing home she worked at. On her way out, she saw me as she touched my hand she asked, "How are you?" I thought she knew I was a patient. I replied, "Not so good." With that response she dropped my hand with a shocked and frightened look on her face and without saying good-bye rushed to the exit to be buzzed out. She looked behind her to see if I was following her. I felt ashamed and worried that she was going to rush back to work to tell the leadership team that I was in the hospital. I was also shocked at her reaction because of her occupation but maybe it is different when you know the person.

She didn't understand that all people on this unit were not crazy. I felt so upset that it ruined my Task Skill group that I looked forward to all day. As I entered the room Sue, teacher, was there and as I got my supplies I had tears in my eyes. I tried to hold them back but I felt so sick I had to release them. Sue asked, "What is wrong?" as I was zoning out again with tears streaming down my cheeks. I told her that I am sad that my previous coworker, Tiffany, treated me the way she did. I was scared she was going to tell everyone that I was here and crazy. Sue tried to ease my anxiety and panic by telling me she is bound to HIPPA law to keep confidentiality. I told her that doesn't matter to them because they like to gossip, right or wrong it doesn't matter. It also would be hard to prove it was her.

I continued in silence while I completed the two projects: 1. a picture of me in the center and all around me were phrases that I hoped someday I would really believe/feel about myself and other goals I hope to see while engaged in the healing process. When I was finished with it I explained it to Sue and she was impressed with my work. 2. I then colored a flower in bright colors. I felt hope after I was finished.

I went back to my room and began to cry again. Tiffany was still on my mind and my anxiety and depression took over as I couldn't stop sobbing. I felt sick and could taste vomit in my mouth. The nurses tried to help me as they saw me struggling. Laura said, "The abusive work environment is in the past. You no longer have a relationship with those people. You have the power to heal yourself. You have to make the decision not to let it bother you. You need to let it go." I felt the nurse didn't understand. They think it is so easy to turn the switch off and not to let it bother me but it is not that simple. I remember the horrible things they did to make me quit.

Then the phone rang and it was my boss, Jenny. I started to cry and I told her why I was upset and felt abused as a woman in the workplace working in a man's world. She told me to remember you didn't have to see those people anymore. It is in the past, you need to let it go to become healthy" I felt a lot better after talking to her.

I soon became upset again as I am lying in my bed motionless and zoning out. I ended up going to the nurses' station and asked for my Depakote and sleeping pill a little earlier. I was so proud of myself because I recognized the emotions and noticed the need for medication. This was progress.

My sister Sonya & Andie called and I gave them the update on my condition. I discussed being bipolar with Andie. I told her what triggers me and where I thought the sources came from. I read her many chapters in my book. She said, "I am so impressed with your writing." She said, the chapters you wrote sucked me in and I don't want you to stop reading." I said," to be continued," and we both laughed.

Later, Phil, Andie's fiancé, called to check up on me and share his troubles of PTSD. He told me in the beginning it is really hard but it is worth it now because he feels good. I felt so supported by my family because they cared enough to keep calling from New York and sharing their own personal struggles which helped me know there will be an end to my misery.

Then I had Ramone, Sabrina, Veronica and Kota, come to visit me for a half an hour. They were crabby. Ramone was tired and worn out. I told him, "Honey, you look tired. You should go home." He replied, "Are you sure?" I told him I was and he seemed relieved to leave as he quickly kissed me good-bye.

Day 6- Mary 16, 2011
I woke up and had my breakfast and felt more alive than the last few days. The previous days, I felt drunk, staggering along and dizzy in a daze. Today, was different because I was a little more alert.

Then I went to Coping Skill class. This time we learned how to use the ABCDEFG Planner. We had to identify the problem by identifying what you want.

What is the problem?—Financial problems. I am behind in bills so in order to try to pay my bills I have to take out quick cash loans to feed my family.

What do you want? 1. To be able to not depend on the quick cash loans for food. 2. To be able to have fun but maybe try to find free events we can do together as a family. 3. Make payments on my doctor bills by setting a goal for $5 each because I have 30 bills and am in $20,000 in debt. 5. To stop helping my parents with money for food.

What's your attitude? 1. My attitude is that I scored it a 1, hopeless. My commitment to solving the problems I scored a 10 because I have the intense desire to make changes and to be successful.

What's the challenge? To use my Business Administration Bachelors to manage my money differently and more effectively. **What activities could help you meet that challenge?** 1. I could stop doing date night with my husband. 2. I could continue working on getting a promotion and a wage increase. 3. Lower my anxiety by doing the bills once every two weeks instead of looking at them all the time. 4. Eat out less and prepare most meals at home.

How or when will you carry out your plan? How many times? By when? For how long? 1. I will try to carry out my plan when I go home. I have learned that 6-8 soda (20oz) a day isn't healthy and I lived without it while staying at the hospital. I hope I will only take one or two times to change my patterns and keep to the routine the rest of my life.

How will you reward yourself? I used to eat large amount of unhealthy food to reward myself but maybe I could go on a date once a month to reconnect with my husband instead.

At the end of class, I told Sue that I was going home but learned a lot. Sue said, "I think you will go home tomorrow sometime." She gave me many other coping ideas to take home with me and told me to keep going on my healing journey.

I went to bed that night and knew I had to go home sometime during the day but hoped it would be after a few more groups. I really enjoyed learning and applying what I learned.

Day 7—May 17, 2011- First Day Home—Discharged at 3:15 p.m.

I ate scrambled eggs and bacon for breakfast and then had my last Coping Skills group. This time I colored a picture of a flower with many details. Sue was happy to see me one last time. I told her I think today will be the day that I will be going home.

I met with the psychiatrist and told him I had a more positive attitude and feel more like myself. I told him the Task Skills and Coping Skills groups were helping me learn. I talked about the medications again because I still felt dizzy. He said, "You can space them out when you take the pills, if that would help." He agreed to lower my dosage on the sleeping pills again. He asked "So are you ready to go home today?" I really wanted to stay another day but the psychiatrist said he was confident it was time to go home, to start healing and reach out to all the support and resources I had available to me. So I agreed.

After the psychiatrist left, the nurse came in and told me it was time for Psycho Therapy Group. We worked on a worksheet called *"Belief Systems—A Powerful Way to Manage Feelings and Behaviors"* by Steve Cavness, PH.D.

We worked on indentifying current feelings we were having and mine were: sad, scared, and ashamed. 2. Identify old self statements: I am falling apart. I am out of control and it is ruining my life. 3. Writing a life events statement: neglect, unsupervised, survived on my own, no parental guidance, sexual, emotional and physical abuse. Injures from being unsupervised, low self-esteem, and depression." 4. My behaviors were getting triggered and I yelled and blamed my family for how I felt because

Flashbacks in Post-Traumatic Stress Disorder: Surviving the Flood

I couldn't cope and I didn't understand what was happening or why I was so angry. 5. My new self statement was: I have a lot of problems and get overloaded but I have strength and resources to heal. 6. The new behavior is: healthy eating, exercise and, release of emotions so I can handle my triggers in a healthier way, being in control to live my life to the fullest.

Before the session ended the psychiatrist told us to look at the bad behaviors and tear that bumper sticker off, as he called it, and replace it with a new improved bumper sticker that has positive behaviors or goals on it. He said, "Let go of the negative by concentrating on the positive."

As the group ended I was so excited to write about this wonderful experience. I rushed to my room to journal. A short time later, the nurse came in and said, "Leslie do you realize you didn't eat." I lost track of time and it was 1:20 p.m. I went and ate my cool meal but I ate fast so I could get to writing some more.

A while went by and it was Task Skills group time. Today I decided to color a backpack w/drawing and writing what it meant to be a survivor. I was just getting started when I was taken out of the group because the social worker wanted to meet with me to discuss discharge paperwork.

The first thing she asked is "How are you doing?" I replied, "I am better and I explained what my trauma was about. She asked if I ever went to the police. I told her no because I had repressed memories for 32 years. I told her of my plan to report my rape to the police and her advice was to wait until I was stronger and to first work on myself. She suggested going back to the abuse center to get further support. She said to ask one of the women to go with me to report so I'm not alone. That was good advice but I knew what I was going to do and it would be immediately. She asked me to sign some release forms. Then she explained my follow up appointments and medications. She asked, "Is there anything else I can do for you?" I told her "No" and thanked her for listening.

I called Emma and asked her to bring me to work so I could hand my FMLA paperwork and my timecard in and that Ramone would pick me up from there.

When Ramone arrived I was so excited to be out of the hospital. The kids were with him and they wanted to go to McDonalds to celebrate me getting out of the hospital. I was only in there for six days but wow it seemed a lot longer. I agreed we would go to McDonalds then after that I had to go to the pharmacy.

I felt confident walking into the pharmacy with the intention to get my medications. I was feeling great after six days in the hospital that I didn't care about being on medications. I used to think I was weak if I admitted I needed help. I was always scared of what people would think and the stigma of mental illness. While I was in the hospital the nurses would talk to me and the coping teacher, Sue, talked to me. They told me it is okay to need medications because I'm getting help for myself. Help is the most important thing because I'm taking care of myself. What people think about me doesn't matter because they don't experience my suffering while making the rest of my family suffer with me.

I came to the conclusion that I wasn't strong by stuffing my emotions. I was hiding from my problems which affected my family. I realized by admitting myself into crisis care and letting the flashbacks release, talking it out was where the real strength was because I had to trust myself, relive the trauma, have strength to report, and survive if it was too late to prosecute. If I could save future victims then it would be worth it to me. I was relieved as I held my head up high as the pharmacist explained my medications respectfully and without judgment.

I felt like a new person and I felt the overwhelming need to do something for myself. This time, I followed through on it I bought six bras and underwear. I have neglected myself that I only had two bra's at a time and six pairs of underwear at a time. I would replace them in time and it was like this for 11 years. It felt so good to buy myself something for a change.

As I walked to the van, I walked with confidence and joy because I felt like I was starting to change my destructive patterns. The sun shining symbolized "new beginnings." I watched a movie with Ramone and was joking and having a fun time. My husband had a surprise look on his face as he said, "You seem really happy." I replied, "I am really happy." I feel I have hope of surviving all my traumas and can help women and men see the warning signs, triggers, and patterns of abuse. I hope they too can live productive lives and return to work with a sense of control over their emotions.

Chapter 16
Home Sweet Home

Wednesday, May 18, 2011

I woke up the next morning and was so happy because I was in my husband's arms. I felt happy because the coping skills I learned in the hospital were working. It took me months to get back into bed with my husband and to feel safe. I finally, after 6 years, had the desire for sex again. Before this time, I was only able to have sex once a month or once every two months because of my sexual trauma.

I started to journal in the morning and before I knew it was afternoon. I called the psychiatrist contact to get an appointment but it wouldn't be for another five months but the scheduler promised to call me if someone cancelled. I was okay with waiting because the hospital assured me that the psychiatrist that saw me there would continue refilling my medications until I had the opportunity to meet with my permanent psychiatrist.

After that I tried to take my pills and was having problems swallowing the large pill. I started to panic as I choked and almost vomited. I stopped for a moment. I told myself with a few deep breaths that I was safe and that grandma, Maggie, couldn't hurt me anymore. She is deceased and I am safe. When I was calm enough I was able to take my pills.

Friday, May 20, 2011

I felt beautiful, skinny, and comfortable in my body. A man noticed me at the grocery store. He said, "Hi" and then offered to lift the cat litter out of the cart for me. This has never happened to me before. He was friendly and smiles as he told Kota to be good to his momma.

I felt triggers starting to surface. This is when I usually go home and eat an entire bag of chips or go to McDonalds for 3 double cheeseburgers, large fries, and a large coke which makes me feel safe.

I practiced saying to myself "Leslie you're safe. He just likes your smile and likes your presence. He is non-threatening; he is trying to be friendly as well, returning your outgoing behavior."

I was able to calm down, later that day my sister came home and wanted McDonalds and she asked if I wanted anything. I proudly said, "Not today. I'm not going to sabotage myself. Those days are over!" I went to the refrigerator and made myself one cheese toasted sandwich and felt confident I made a good choice. I was taking control back.

I took Veronica to school. Then I went to the store to get some more groceries. Kota and I were checking out we saw a firemen. He said, "Hi, little guy, here is a card with engine #19 with facts on the back as well as a message not to play with matches." When we went outside the fire truck was parked at the curb so I had Kota stand in front of the fire truck as I took a photo. Kota was so excited to show and tell everyone about the firemen and the big fire truck.

Kota rushed into grandma's house and tried to tell them what happened. I told him to slow down and then say it again. He showed the card and the photos on my cell phone. Then I helped him explain. It was an exciting day for him and me.

I used my sister's laptop and checked my email and I got a reply from Stella for the email I sent her the night before. She reassured me of her love, concern, and support. She wanted to help me through the healing process. I sent her another email telling her my needs for validation of what happened to us if she were ready and far enough in her own healing process. I asked if she started her healing journey yet. Then I sent the email to her.

Then it was time for Kota and me to go home on the way we had to stop at the Quick cash store to pay off a loan for $610.00. First, I had to stop at the Tyme machine for $50 more dollars. I had to take out the loan because I was having problems with finances because I was eating out with my kids 2 to 3 times a week I didn't want or have the energy to cook.

Kota and I walked through the doors and he asked as he grabbed my arm with terror "What's that?" I said, "Oh that is the money man. I know you never saw this before but there is no need to be afraid."

The Tyme machine was being serviced and Kota was intrigued of how things work. He watched the older gray haired man open the safe inside and take out the drawers. The man would look on the machine to know how many bills to add to each drawer. Kota had one hand on the safe inside the machine. He was getting too close to the man, as I reminded him to please back up. "The man smiled and said; "As long as he doesn't take samples, we'll be all right," as he laughed. This was another new memory we could put in the positive experiences. I felt like there were guardian angels showing me that people can be good and they are not always abusive.

When he was finished he put the machine back together and waited for the machine to confirm amounts were verified and rebooted the screen. He offered a friendly good-bye as Kota gave him a high five.

Then we went to the Quick cash store and then home to make supper. Once home I decided to give the complete control over to my 15 year old daughter, Sabrina, so she can experience how difficult a woman's schedule can be. She was so excited because I wouldn't let her cook because I was so stressed and nervous that I had to have control all the time.

I was standing there as Veronica walked into the kitchen with an open nail polish bottle and I told her to leave right now. Nail polish and remover is a trigger. My husband started to see panic in my eyes as he escorted Veronica out of the kitchen.

I finished telling Sabrina I was so proud of her that she was maturing and that dad would be nearby if she needed any help or had any questions. She was making ground turkey burritos with green pepper, spinach, black beans, onion, chick peas and cheese.

I told Ramone I needed to go talk to Veronica and have some time with her. But noticed I didn't feel well because of the incident in the kitchen with the nail polish. It reminded me of my grandmother's, Maggie, abuse.

I talked with Veronica as a check in basis and asked if any new flashbacks surfaced for her. She said, "No." She asked, "Can I practice my lines for my play, mom?" I replied, sure but as she was talking and singing I felt faint and dizzy which I have experienced before. I asked, "Is it okay if I take a nap first," "Sure mommy," with a smile. I was so tired all of a sudden so I closed my eyes while telling the "child within", "Honey, it is okay Grandma can't hurt you anymore. She is dead. You are safe. I love you and will protect you." The next thing I remember is my daughter, Sabrina, jerking my arm yelling, "Mommy it is time to try my supper." I said "I'll be there in a minute" as I slowly got up and felt a lot better.

Sabrina looked so confident and hospitable as she served everyone their meal. She explained she used the cookbook and followed all the directions but confessed that dad did the measuring for the spices because "I didn't want to screw it up." At that moment I felt sad because I realized that she always wanted to cook with me and do the mother-daughter cook day. I was so stressed out all the time and nervous in the kitchen. I needed all the control so it prevented me from cooking with her because I was triggered in the kitchen with memories of my ex-husband criticizing my meals and telling me it was no good and leaving his plate on the table and leaving to go eat at a bar.

Everything was starting to make sense to me because I felt good on medication. Each day I saw things more clearly while continuing to heal.

I told Sabrina the burritos tasted awesome. I explained, "I would like your help. We wouldn't have to wait so long for supper to be done." I said, "Sometimes doing prep work would help and sometimes a full meal, we will see." She was so excited and felt pride, confidence and loved as she said "I love you mom."

I also felt so awesome because I finally delegated something. That was a huge step for me.

After supper, Veronica asked if we wanted to play a game. Sabrina said, "Okay what's the game?" She said, "It's a riddle game I made up."

Riddle 1: Little kids like to sing about me, even adults and teens. There are 26 of me. I make up millions of stuff. I can be big or small or tall or short or light or dark. What am I? The answer is the letters of the alphabet.

Riddle 2: I am brown with silver on me about a size of a regular piece of paper. Maybe a tad bit bigger. I am hard so you can write on me. What am I? The answer is a clip board.

Riddle 3: I am an important part of your body. I protect pink organs. I am hard as a rock even harder. What am I? The answer is your skull.

We were laughing and being playful. I was so happy I could see healing taking place. I realized I needed to do something for myself so I ended the evening with a nice candle light bath.

Part Seven
Healing Continues

Chapter 17
Affects on Family Relationships

Day out with the kids:

The kids wanted to go to a fast food restaurant. After I ordered, I stepped back with a group of customers waiting to pick up their food. I was keeping a watch on the kids filling up their drinks. This guy next to me said, "Those three kids aren't all your kids are they?" I laughed, "They sure are." He returned with, "The miracle grow must have been working." His food came and he said, "Have a nice day." I replied, "You too."

The girls and I sat down and were enjoying our food as we talked about going to the craft store. I wanted to start having craft activities at home to help reconnect with the kids. It would be a coping activity as well, when any of us were triggered and needed our mind off of it.

My daughter, Veronica, 13 years old, then makes the comment to me that the "Guy was flirting with you before. Oh I wonder what dad would say?" I knew it was a joke as I gave her a fake smile. She laughed playfully as a little schoolgirl would.

I felt sick as if I needed to go to the bathroom. I could tell I was going to have some type of episode. As I was sitting on the toilet, my stomach started to hurt like it has done before then I felt a severe and burning pain in my anus. It felt like something was ripping out. I started to cry because it hurt badly but by being in the hospital they told me this is a body memory. I started to calmly tell my "child within" "You are safe, no one will hurt you, and the bad people are gone." This is just a memory in the past it is not happening right now." "You are okay." "You will get through this." After I did this I felt better.

I took the kids out to the van and told them "I have to go home because mom is feeling ill." "My daughter, Veronica, 13 years old, said with concern, "Mom are you okay?" as she put her hand on my shoulder. Sabrina is screaming, "I knew it you are breaking another promise, just like you always do." Veronica is yelling at her to "Shut up Mom is ill." I told Veronica it is okay that Sabrina doesn't know what we are going through because her therapy is slower than ours.

I tried to explain to Sabrina that I am triggered. She didn't care all she cared about was that she got her own way. This is because by me breaking a promise it triggered her "child within" and she reverted back to a 3 year old. Her dad always made promises her couldn't keep. Kota, 4 years old, is just soaking it all in. I am so worried for him and think he will be the next one to go into therapy.

I told everyone, "to just give me a few minutes," as I rested my head on the steering wheel while doing my breathing exercises, trying to lessen the dizziness and bring the anxiety level down. After a short time, I thought I could continue to fulfill my promise to Kota, Sabrina and Veronica by taking them to the craft store.

When we arrived at the craft store the kids were excited. They had to hurry to make their selection because the store was closing in 20 minutes. Sabrina tried to talk to me about getting our art supplies but I couldn't engage her, as I was dizzy trying not to faint. We walked slowly to the check out as the store clerk announced they were closing. Everyone loaded up into the van as I told the kids once more, "I needed a little bit of time to do some deep breathing exercises to lower my anxiety." This time no one objected.

When I reached my mom's house, the kids rushed into the dining room to play with the items they bought at the craft store. I walked into the living room where my mom and sister, Victoria, were sitting. Without saying a word, I went into my mom's room and lay on the bed. My mom came in and said, "Honey, are you okay?" I told her I am having body memories. She asked, "What is that?" I told her, "It is when your body experiences the abuse at this moment instead of being in the past." "My body doesn't recognize it happened in the past so it is making me feel it right now." "My mom said, "I have never gone through this." "I am so sorry honey," as she held me. I fell asleep for about 2 ½ hours before waking up and feeling better. The dizziness was gone.

I went home and told my husband what happened. He took me in his arms and held me and told me, "I am so sorry you are going through this." I said, "I think we better slow things down with us." I was so excited my sexual desire came back after 6 years that we were intimate twice since I got home from the hospital. I said, "I think I am going too fast." He told me, "That is okay." "I will do whatever you need me to do," as he kissed the top of my head and then my lips. I felt so much love and safety at that moment. The anxiety seemed to pass and I felt like it was a small victory because I got through it with the coping skills I learned from the hospital. I also didn't have to go to the ER in a panic from the pain I was experiencing from body memories. Now that I knew what was happening to me I knew it would blow over in time. I started to feel better as I had supper with my husband and we decided to cozy up and watch a movie, as the kids were at their grandparent's house.

Panic episode while at a family picnic:

My daughter, Sabrina, had a picnic for her school choir that we all were invited to participate. All the choirs, orchestra, and band students from all the schools would be there. We were so excited to go and we bought tickets ahead of time. I looked forward to the picnic all day. I was excited to have some fun family time. When we got there we ate right away and there was music entertainment that was loud but I seemed to be okay with it. After everyone was done eating, it was time to play on the playground.

My son ran one way and my two daughters the other way. My husband, Ramone, watched Kota as I watched my daughters from a distance. Mother's are not cool. As I stood there looking at all the children having fun with their parents, I felt sad because I never had that opportunity with my parents when I was little. I started to scan the crowd to look for Stella's dad to make sure he wasn't there. I started to smell an overwhelming odor of wood chips as my awareness of the smell increased I felt sick, dizzy, and panicked. I had to flee to get out of the danger zone quickly. I waved frantically for my family to come as I said, "We have to go now!" As I started to run toward the car, Sabrina was screaming at me that she didn't want to go. Veronica also didn't want to go. Ramone collected Kota and met me at his car.

Sabrina still screaming as I am telling her I am triggered again by the wood chips and told her what I was feeling. Veronica yelled, "Sabrina shut up mom is having problems", as she tried to comfort me. "Mom, are you okay?" "Mom, look at me and breathe! You're safe." "Your trauma is not happening now it is in the past." I was able to calm myself down but didn't want to go back to the picnic.

Veronica asked very calmly "Can we go somewhere just the girls?" Sabrina said, "No Veronica mom won't do that either." She was so sassy because her dad was telling her that the counselors were putting false memories in my head.

We agreed to go out for ice cream. We each ordered our favorite ice cream treat and sat down. I was calm and had no more triggers at that point. So I said, "Happily what would you girls like to talk about?" Sabrina negatively and angry said "I told you everything I had to say at the park." "You wreck my fun every time." "You never want me to have fun." "You hate me." "I always trigger you." I tried to explain to her it is something in my environment that causes me to panic not her. It is the way you act when I am in crisis that is difficult to handle. I went home and slept for 1 ½ hours.

Leslie's counseling session with Sandy—Discussed Stella's Dad and brother panic episodes.

Sandy greeted me like always as we walked back to her office. I sat on the couch ready to get down to business. I always had a list of items I want to work on. The list was items that came up since our last appointment. I started to tell her and she told me to wait as she put the EMDR headsets on me with soft music playing and found our brain spot which holds the place where the trauma was being stored, before continuing. We also picked a focal point and something that made me feel safe. I picked God holding the little girl.

Then she told me to continue as I first told her about the first situation at the restaurant. She asked me the question, "What number of an age comes to mind." "Don't think about it. Just say what first pops in to your mind." I answered "6 years old." "She started by asking, "What do you think made you feel dizzy, tired, and sick from your childhood." I replied, "We sometimes didn't have food for days so I felt weak and I would go to bed hungry." She then asked, "What about that man didn't you trust?" She told me to let the 6-year-old answer. She told me to pay attention to images, smells, or how my body felt.

I said," I feel fear, as the flashbacks started. Stella's brother would come in the room and scare us, break our dolls, and shoving us, before sexually abusing us." Then afterwards he would leave us alone to play the rest of the afternoon, allowing us to be little girls." I also talked about finding God at 6 years old. Stella's Mom, Anne, took me to her church and had me participate in choir, bible camp, Sunday school, and learned about God's love. Sandy repeated the question, "What about that man didn't you trust?"

Then I had a flashback of Stella's dad, Jack, "Stella's dad thought he was charming by smiling as his cheeks seemed to shine with a perverted look on his face, while I witnessed him fingering his daughter, Stella on the playground on the monkey bars. "As he kept repeating "Daddy loves you, tickle, tickle, tickle." Throughout this process Sandy would remind me to breathe in through my nose and release through my mouth. She also told me to do whatever I needed to feel comfortable with my body. Then Sandy asked me to ask the 6-year-old little girl if this is at a good place to stop. I told her that no the little girl wants to go on to the next situation that happened at the picnic because she thinks they are connected.

Sandy said "Okay". I continued to explain about the wood chips, the overwhelming odor, and panic to flee the immediate danger. I also explained Sabrina's reaction to me. Then again flashbacks started and brought me back to Stella's dad abusing her on the playground, while I witnessed in terror. I remember seeing the wood chips below me and could smell them again as I felt the need to flee. My legs felt like running so I started to gesture a running motion. My arms were tingly so I shook them. I was breathing in and out and was unable to say anything but I needed to. I felt pressure in my stomach. So I used my sign language to say "No more silence." Then I yelled the words "You are safe now!" The police know about him. "I reported it for you honey." "He can't hurt you no more." Sandy asked me if there was anything else the little girl needed to say. I said, "She needs validation from Stella and for her to be okay too." Sandy responded, "You can't be in charge of healing anyone but yourself." I responded," I should have been able to protect her." "I was a little older than she was." Sandy replied, "Honey you were just a baby, you couldn't have stopped it on your own." We closed the session and talked about the experience. I felt so good because some of the body memories and panic were released.

Motorcycle—Panic Episode:

I was enjoying my Saturday morning with my son. It was sunny with blue skies. I had the doors open the birds were singing and Kota, age 4, was putting his puzzle together on his desk and I was journaling on my computer, nothing could have been better. I could tell today would be a good day.

From a distance, I heard motorcycles coming towards my house. This has occurred so many times before and never bothered me. The motorcycle gang has their place nearby. As they passed the house one by one, I remembered my rapist, Bret, and what happened and the fact he told me his dad belonged to this motorcycle gang.

I became panicked and took Kota in my arms yelling "We have to get out of here right now!" I grabbed him abruptly taking him away from his puzzle, safety, and grabbed my purse, the keys and ran out the door. I felt the motorcycle gang was after us and we were in immediate danger. My son was crying because I scared him. We were still in our pj's.

I reached my mom's house panicking and crying as she tried to calm me down, as I was telling her, "I don't want to return to my house." I think, "Bret found me mom!" "If he did, we are in danger. I don't want him to hurt my daughters the same way." My sister took my son and was talking to him trying to reassure him he is safe and that mommy is okay.

Counseling Session with Sandy- Motorcycle Panic Episode:

Sandy started the session with asking how I was doing. I told her about the panic attack when the motorcycles passed my house. I told her about the dizzy spells and that I get extremely tired and have to sleep for 1 or 2 hours then I wake up refreshed. She suggested we change our appointment schedule to every other week and then have art therapy with Cindy on opposite weeks to break up the trauma sessions. Sandy explained that this would help me cope better. The dizzy spells followed by fatigue are more ego-states coming through that will surface new memories or triggers to deal with.

Chapter 18
The Psychiatrist

First Visit

My first visit to the psychiatrist's office, I looked inside the large hospital and started to panic. I felt warm and my heart started to beat fast as I looked around and didn't see anyone I recognized. I was standing in the middle of the lobby and circling around trying to read signs but none of them looked familiar. Then a gentle older woman's voice from the help desk said, "Can I help you, honey?" "Do you know where you need to go?" I felt relieved to see a friendly face. I replied with shame and embarrassment while whispering, "Yes, Behavioral Health, please." She told me the directions and saw that I had a frightened look on my face as I looked up toward the ceiling. She said "You know what? I can just take you there." "I need to walk a little anyway my legs hurt if I sit too long." I thanked her as we walked down the hall. We got as far as the elevator and she said with a compassionate smile "It's on 5th floor. Can you find your way?" I replied with a thankful sigh of relief, "Yes I can find it now."

As I thanked her for helping me, she extended her kindness again. She told me if I needed help to come back down, I could have someone call her and she would come and get me. I thanked her as I pushed the button. I had tears in my eyes as I saw her walk away because she was such a nice lady and seemed to have no judgment in her eyes as she looked at me. I saw wisdom of life, concern, compassion, and understanding of what I was going through.

The elevator doors opened and I cautiously stepped inside. I pushed the number five and watched the elevator door close. I was so nervous and had a thousand thoughts running through my mind about how the visit would go. Would I like the psychiatrist, would he put me back into the hospital or tell me I am crazy, etc? The elevator reached the 5th floor. As the door opened, I see in large letters Behavioral Health Department. I stepped out with my head bowed as if I was waiting for people in white coats to jump out, grab me or hit me over the head with a club and carry me away to a secret room never to be seen again.

As I stepped off the elevator none of those things happened, of course not, how silly. I turned to the right and carefully read the sign in front of the receptionist desk, "Please form a line at this point to protect the confidentiality of our patients." I was proud to stand right there for my turn. I thought to myself, "Wow they offer respect to me as their patient, even before I am seen. I think I will like it here."

A woman said, "Come forward, it is your turn. What can I do for you today?" I whispered I am here to see Dr. Peterson. She said okay with a smile, "What is your name?" I replied Leslie Raddatz, as I look around to see if anyone I knew was there. She then took my insurance information and asked me to repeat my contact information. Then she said, "Okay Leslie you may sit down and the nurse will be right with you." I took a deep breath and stepped to my left to find a spot.

I saw several patients waiting and it felt as if they were all staring at me so I picked a chair that was facing the television. I was looking at the television and I heard the clock go tick tock tick tock. I saw many patients go in and out. I knew my turn would eventually come but I was one hour early. I wanted to be there on time so my anxiety of driving wouldn't make me late. I left two hours early from work. It took me one hour to go 30 miles and find a parking spot to park the van. I was afraid I'd have a panic attack that it would completely paralyze me and I wouldn't be able to move without calling my husband to help.

Flashbacks in Post-Traumatic Stress Disorder: Surviving the Flood

I heard the door open and the nurse finally called my name. I took my time gathering my items as my heart was beating out of my chest. I was sweating and terrified as I looked at the other patients, as I passed by them. The nurse looked at me and said, "You were early today. Sorry for the wait." I joked and told her it was the construction that I was worried about but that wasn't true because the route I took didn't have construction yet.

She led me into her office where she asked me for a list of medications. She took care of the insurance, release papers, and explained med refill policies. Then she took my blood pressure and weight. She seemed very nice and I felt comfortable with her. I was starting to get calm until she asked me the dreaded question: "Why do you need to see Dr. Peterson?"

There we go again panic set in as I tried to keep my breathing under control. I told her that I was referred from my physician to a counselor, Sandy. Then Sandy told me I needed a psychiatrist but no one was taking new patients. Then my regular physician, instructed me to go into the hospital in crisis care and that they would be forced to evaluate me with the psychiatrist on-call. They would also be forced to prescribe medications, until I could find my permanent psychiatrist. I had good luck when I got a call that Dr. Peterson was relocating his practice and he was taking new patients. She said, "Okay, honey you can relax and take a deep breath," as she put he hands on mine. "What are the issues you need help with?"

I explained that I was already diagnosed with PTSD (post-traumatic stress disorder) and possibly Bi-polar. I told her I wanted a second opinion on bipolar because I didn't believe that a doctor could sit with me for five minutes in crisis care and give me a proper diagnosis. I reminded her I was put on medications: Depakote ER 1000 MG for Bi-polar, Effexor XR 150 MG for anxiety and depression, Trazodone

50MG sleeping pills, and Losartan/HCTZ 50/12.5 mg for my high blood pressure. She asked, "Why are you on these meds?" There was no more hiding the reasons why. I started to half breakdown bowed my head in shame, and tears started as I told her I was neglected by my parents, never felt loved, molested by my friend's relatives and my great uncle Charlie. Then I was raped at 14 years old, and then had an abusive marriage that ended in divorce.

I told her I was scared because of all my medical issues and that I need help which is very difficult for me to admit. Then I apologized for being emotional. She told me not to apologize, "Leslie, you have really been through a lot in your life." "It sounds like you are on the right path with counseling, taking your medications and now you are here." She commented "You will like Dr. Peterson. He is very nice." She wrote some notes for Dr. Peterson and then got out of her chair and told me that he would be right with me and to take care of myself. It will get better.

A few moments later, a man in dress clothes appeared in the doorway and asked me to come with him. It was Dr. Peterson, I guess I expected him in a white coat and remembered my imagery when I was getting off the elevator. I laughed at myself inside as I thought, "Well, they are more sneaky, if they are in plain clothes. I'll have to keep a look out." I chuckled again as I realized how silly my thoughts were.

As we walk into his office, I commented on his office view and how beautiful his days must be with the view out the huge windows. I told him how depressed I get in winter without the sunlight. He commented that we may need to get a special light for me during those difficult times. I am a very outgoing person to strangers until the view points to me or my problems. He asked me to take a seat. He started by introducing himself as Dr. Peterson and I told him my name. He asked, "What can I do for you?"

Flashbacks in Post-Traumatic Stress Disorder: Surviving the Flood

I started by telling him I was in counseling at *New Beginnings Counseling Center* with Sandy since March. She diagnosed me with PTSD and that my regular physician, Dr. Anderson, was the one who referred me to Sandy. She feels it is time for me to get a psychiatrist to get medication to help me through the difficult trauma issues I am dealing with.

I also shared that I was in the hospital in May for a week and that a psychiatrist at the hospital diagnosed me with bi-polar but I asked Dr. Peterson for a second opinion. He said "Okay, we can do that." "What has happened in your life to get you admitted to the hospital?"

As I told him what I told his nurse he wrote detailed notes. Then he asked questions: "Have you ever been in a psychiatric hospital? I replied, "No."

"Did you go to college?" I was proud to tell him I had four degrees: Office Assistant and Administrative Assistant degree from the technical college and a Bachelor of Arts in Business Administration and Bachelor of Arts in Marketing from a four-year college. "Have you ever been convicted of a crime or arrested?" I replied "No," with a giggle. "How are you at work?" I was proud to tell him that I was just promoted and that this was the fourth promotion in eight years and that the salary increase was more than I ever imagined for my entire career. He nodded and smiled and asked, "How are relationships with family members and others?" I told him of the neglect and injuries I endured as a child from poor supervision and the fact I never felt loved by my mom and dad. I also told him about being molested, raped, force fed by grandma. He continued to write a lot of notes.

I also explained that my children also have PTSD because of an abusive ex- husband. They suffered a lot of emotional, physical and sexual trauma as well. I told him of the struggles to try and limit his contact with the girls through the courts, social workers and police and that so far it has been unsuccessful. I told him of my hopes of them being able to cope better than me because I have them in counseling with Sandy and in art therapy. He said, "I have a great amount of respect for you because other parents allow the patterns to repeat over and over again." He said, "But you got them into counseling at an early age. They will have a better chance at a normal life. They will develop the coping skills needed to cope with their PTSD."

"How is your health?" Then I replied "Not good at all because weird occurrences happen to me and the doctors have no answers and are very rude to me at times." He said, "What weird occurrences?" I told him, "I am scared you will think I am crazy but here goes:"

Reoccurring illnesses—colds, bronchitis, migraine headaches. I also have high blood pressure and am obese weighing 215 pounds and am a size 18W.

PTSD Symptoms—panic attacks, anxiety, zoning out, nervousness, certain smells and sounds bother me. I have constant triggers to deal with that is affecting my entire life.

Training for Half-Marathon—I developed hives so severe that my entire face swelled to such an extent that if you knew me you wouldn't have recognized me. I also had large welts on my back and arms.

Training for Half-Marathon—While using the run/walk method, I had heart problems. I had to lie on the side of the road because my heart rate went from 140 to 220 in seconds. I felt like I was having a heart attack because my chest was hurting and I felt faint and dizzy. I was so scared. I went to ER and they ordered a stress test and did blood tests and found nothing. They told me to keep exercising and it probably happened due to me still being out of shape.

Flashbacks in Post-Traumatic Stress Disorder: Surviving the Flood

Movie Story—I had severe abdominal pain so I went to the bathroom. I had cold sweats, diarrhea and pain in my anus and felt an eerie feeling like I needed to get into a public area. I pulled my pants up and walked into the lobby to ask for help. I ended up passing out and woke up with hives everywhere. The manager of the movie theater called 911 and the ambulance arrived and took me to the hospital. The doctor took blood tests to make sure I wasn't diabetic. I told them the tests have all been done before and that the doctors before them didn't find anything but they insisted in taking the blood tests anyway. I was right. They couldn't explain what happened to me. They gave me fluids and sent me home.

Stomach Pain & Nausea—I get horrible pain in my stomach and then I feel like I have to vomit and I try to resist it but ultimately I end up vomiting. After 17 hours of enduring this pain, I return back to normal. I used to go to the ER for this too before I knew how to deal with it. I thought I had a stomach tumor or ulcer. I also get the diarrhea during this stressful time but it also disappears when I vomit. When I went to the ER they gave me nausea and pain pills and it passed over.

Department Store Story—I got a sharp pain in my eye. Then I had severe memory loss, and was unable to speak or read, I felt confused, and my body went numb. I didn't even know my name, husband, or son or the date, president, or year. I was taken to the ER and discussed my symptoms with the doctor. I mentioned my friend had a stroke a month ago so I came in, just in case. He told me he would do some blood tests and would be back in. As he left, the door was still open a crack. My husband and I overheard the doctor say to the nurses that her friend had a stroke so now she thinks she is having one. They all had a big laugh. I looked at my husband who I still didn't remember and I started to cry. I felt like they didn't believe what I told him. My husband tried to comfort me but I was still scared of him because I didn't remember him.

After the test results came in the doctor said there was nothing unusual in your blood tests. It was a possible ATI, small stroke, or a confusion migraine. Then for three weeks other symptoms were present along with more doctor visits to specialists with no resolution. I was on Family Medical Leave from work for three weeks. After resting for three weeks at home my symptoms seem to disappear and I went back to work.

Dr. Peterson looked at me in astonishment and said, "You have been through a lot and you are doing so well in all aspects of your life while struggling with PTSD, anxiety, and depression and the health issues." He looked at me and with a smile he said, "I can tell you what is happening to you and it is fixable with medication. I asked, "Am I crazy?" He replied, "No you are not crazy." I was so relieved because I started to think it was all in my head. He said, "No you have PTSD (post-traumatic stress disorder) and also you have what is called conversion and somatization which are both anxiety disorders."

Dr. Peterson told me the technical definitions and then explained them to me in simpler terms.

PTSD (post-traumatic stress disorder)—Because of the traumas I experienced in my life, I developed PTSD and that is why my symptoms surface such as panic attacks, anger outbursts, dizziness, startling easily, trouble sleeping, nightmares, flashbacks, body memories, and more.

Conversion Disorder—When I am triggered and am experiencing a lot of stress then my body, brain, legs, arms, stomach, etc. are affected by experiencing the symptoms of abnormal pain, vomiting, sexual dysfunction, trouble sleeping, sharp pain in my eyes, confusion, memory loss, and more.

Somatization Disorder—This disorder can explain my physical complaints and why I go to the doctors several times for help with my symptoms, such as my nausea, bloating, diarrhea, and sensitivities to certain food, pain while having sex, lack of sex interest, headaches, my back and join pain, difficulty swallowing or speaking, urinary retention, numbness in my arms and tingly fingers, seizures, my legs giving out on me and running into walls as I walk through doorways. With all these symptoms, the tests don't show anything wrong with me. The doctors are not able to diagnose me with a specific illness.

Dr. Peterson said, "Yes, all can be explained by your three anxiety disorders you have. The disorders can occur concurrently and that is why you get overwhelmed with your daily activities, environment, family, body, etc. This is why you feel triggered with, anxiety, nervousness, and always feel like you are under the fight or flight mode."

I looked at him with tears in my eyes because someone finally had all the answers and the fact he confirmed that I am not CRAZY. These symptoms are occurring and I have the right to feel the way I do when it occurs. I asked, "Are my disorders life threatening and will I have them for the rest of my life?" He replied, "PTSD you will probably have the rest of your life but the other two will be limited or disappear if the PTSD is controlled."

I explained with tears and dismay how the doctors treated me so rudely like I was wasting their time when I go into the ER in a panic from my symptoms. He said, "Now that you are diagnosed with these disorders they should be more understanding and treat you with respect." He went into action as he went into his computer to change my diagnoses. I asked, "So I don't have bi-polar?" He replied, "No, you were right. You are not bi-polar!" I was so relieved and felt so much joy inside. I could have jumped out of my chair. I said excitedly "What are the next steps?" He said, "The first thing we will do is take you off the Depakote because that is for bi-polar and you are not bi-polar. The second is to increase the Effexor from 150 mg to 225 mg for anxiety and depression." He asked, "How are the sleeping pills working?" I replied, "I have more nightmares and I am constantly tossing and turning." He said, "Okay I will prescribe a different sleeping pill called Zolpidem 5 mg, 1 pill per night for sleeping."

He asked if his nurse explained the procedure for refilling medications and I told him yes. He commented that he feels I am on the right path and to keep going because I am doing a great job. He walked me down the hallway to the scheduling office. He told the receptionist to schedule a follow-up in a month. I felt I was finally in good hands. I thanked him for all the insight today because I felt a lot better about what was happening. He replied, "You will feel better in a few weeks when the medication starts to work."

I got on the elevator and pressed the first floor button, as I remembered what the nice woman said to me. When the doors opened, I took a deep breath. I looked to my left then to my right and chose to turn left. As I walked down the hallway I saw the help desk and felt proud that I made it by myself. I stopped at the help desk and thanked the woman who helped me find my way and wished her to a happy rest of her day. She thanked me for stopping and said, "She would see me the next time I come." As I was going to find my car it occurred to me that she probably doesn't get much recognition for her job. I felt even better that I probably made her day happy just like she made mine.

Second Visit
This time the driving, parking, and finding my way to the 5th floor was not a problem because it was all familiar to me. I felt proud of myself as I walked into the door and didn't need the help desk assistance to find my way. The woman who helped me before was there and as our eyes met, she smiled and waved and I returned the gesture. It felt like a very welcoming healing environment.

Flashbacks in Post-Traumatic Stress Disorder: Surviving the Flood

The nurse preformed the routine by asking about my medication. She took my blood pressure, pulse and took my weight. Then she asked, "How are you doing?" I told her, "Not well. My anxiety and nervousness are still bothering me and I am still not sleeping." The tears of defeat and despair surfaced and I apologized, "I am just so overwhelmed with my older kids mistreating me and my new promotion." With an understanding look she said, "Don't apologize, it is okay. Woman these days have a lot of demands put on them and it is difficult to juggle everything." As she walked to the door I said, "Thank you for your understanding." I told her I am grateful for the kindness and comfort she showed me. She replied, "Dr. Peterson will be right with you." I watched her as she left the room with a final good-bye smile.

Dr. Peterson came in and sat in the chair as he asked, "How are you doing?" with a compassionate look on his face. "My anxiety and nervousness are still here." I also told him about my girls and how it is too much to handle with them testing me and their own PTSD issues. Then there's my ex-husband. "I feel guilty for yelling at them because I am trying to be the perfect mom." He looked at me and said, "You are a wonderful mom but no parent is perfect." I told him I knew that but I need to still try. He said, "These are symptoms of your PTSD and we need to get a better control of it."

We agreed that work still needed to be done to control my PTSD, anxiety, depression and nervousness by prescribing Clonazepam 0.5 mg to take twice a day. And new sleeping pills called Zaleplon 5 mg 2 per night. He told me to keep the other medications as they are. He said good-bye and wished me well and gave me comfort by telling me if I have any questions or concerns that I could call his nurse.

Third Visit

On July 18, 2011, I called Dr. Peterson's nurse in a panic because the anxiety, nightmares, stomach pain, vomiting and severe diarrhea was now occurring at work. I was in a panic because I don't want it to start affecting my job. I just was promoted. I also told her how lucky I was that my boss was on vacation for two weeks so I need to get better quickly. She told me she could get me in before Dr. Peterson goes on vacation.

As I drove to my appointment I had high anxiety about driving and whether or not I would be in a car accident. I was anxious when I finally walked into the lobby but the receptionist was there smiling at me as I walked past the help desk, just as before. It seemed like GOD chose her to be my guardian angel to calm me and to let me know I am not alone in my suffering.

The nurse finally called my name and with a sigh of relief I put on a happy face and followed the nurse to her office. The nurse preformed the routine by asking about my medication. She took my blood pressure, pulse and took my weight. Then she asked the question, "How are you doing?" I replied, "It is like I told you on the phone." "Oh yes." She reads her notes from our conversation. She asked if I had any questions for her. I replied, "No!" She said, "The doctor will be in to see you soon but he is running about 15 minutes late." I replied, "That is okay. It gives me time to try and relax." She started toward the door, and I said, "Thank you so much for getting me an appointment today." She replied, "I couldn't bear thinking of you home suffering over the weekend with no help." She saw my face of gratitude before leaving and I saw her smiling so I hope I made her day better.

Dr. Peterson came in and sat down in his chair and said, "Hi, how are things going?" I told him about the rape flashbacks, the feelings of being paranoid because a white car has been parked next to my house in a school parking lot for five weeks with police license plates. The sheriff I talked to was unaware of why it was there. The Sheriff promised to follow up with me and never did.

I said, "I have a worry that the police officer who helped my rapist, Bret, get away with running me over is watching me. I feel like they are going to hurt my family and I feel like I can't protect my children. I have horrible images in my head of Bret raping my daughters."

He asked me if I was working on this issue with my counselor, Sandy, and I told him, "Yes, I talked to Sandy and she helped me do EMDR and Brainspotting Therapy on this issue. I just don't seem to get over this trauma because I think this is the hardest one to get over. I think I have to lose the weight, get self confidence back, and to find ways to stop sabotaging myself so I can get down to 140 pounds and then maybe I can get over this trauma." He said, "That is hard work. You need to start out slow and you can achieve it but be kind to yourself."

Dr. Peterson said that he would suggest another medication called Risperidone 0.5 mg tablets twice a day. He told me that doctors give this drug to the men and women who came back from Vietnam War with severe flashbacks. This should work. "Don't worry I am giving you a small dosage. We will also increase your Clonazepam 0.5 mg to 3 tablets a day. Keep the rest of the pills you are taking as they are prescribed."

I thanked him again and asked if I should keep my next regularly scheduled appointment and he answered, "Yes." I left his office feeling like there is still hope that I could beat this. I beat every other cross God gave me to bear.

Fourth Visit

I checked in at the receptionist desk and sat down and on the television was a show that had doctors talking about the eye and how you can tell what is wrong with your body by looking at the eye and its condition. One thing they talked about was pink eye and another stroke, etc.

The nurse called my name and we went to the office and went through the routine. Shortly after the nurse left Dr. Peterson came and led me to his office. He asked, "How are you?" I told him that I was much better but the Clonazepam makes me really tired and I am unable to function at work. While he was looking up the dosage I was on, I told him of the positives in my life such as me sharing joint custody with my ex-husband which would help lower the stress, having time for myself to exercise, lose weight, and hopefully be a more calmer parent when the girls return home. I told him how hard it was to let go of control which I am doing slowly, first with the girls and then other things would come.

I explained how Kota currently is being affected by the girls, me and Ramone with all the chaos. "I am looking forward to helping Kota work through his tantrums, bed wetting, and hopefully get him to sleep in his own bed before the girls come home. I have plans to have new rules in the house and to make my house a home before the girls get back. I noticed there are no photos of my family on the walls. I just never had the time to focus on finalizing my house since we moved in ten years ago. I have been stuck on survival mode. I am looking forward to really working on myself and reconnecting with Ramone too."

He said, "It sounds like a good plan. When does this take place?" "I said, Hopefully the day after the custody hearing." He told me he would like to see me in two months and to see the progress I have made. He reduced the Clonazepam from 3 to 1 mg a day so that would be .05 mg two times a day.

Then remember the television program I saw in the waiting room. By watching that show my brain must have been thinking overtime on it in my subconscious and I ended up with pink eye two days after my visit. Conversion disorder in action!

Flashbacks in Post-Traumatic Stress Disorder: Surviving the Flood

Fifth Visit

As the nurse called my name I got up and on the way to her examination room, she apologized for forgetting about me for 30 minutes. I told her it was okay because I was watching an interesting Dr. Phil episode. She seemed relieved as we did the routine stuff and she said, "The doctor will be right in to see you." A few minutes later Dr. Peterson appeared in the doorway with a smile and led me to his office.

He asked, "How are you doing?" I started off by thanking him for taking my call on September 2, about the Risperidone side effects scare. He said, "No problem, how are the side effects now? Is your body getting back to normal?" I replied, "Well, my breasts are a cup larger and two sizes bigger but the milk stopped leaking out of my breast. My menstrual cycle hasn't returned yet. I jokingly said, "I am not pregnant. I got a pregnancy test because I was so worried." He reassured me that my period would return once the medication had time to work out of my system. He was amazed that my body acted this way because it was a very rare possibility that these side effects would occur. I told him I have bad luck.

I said, "Did you ever find out what happened with your phone number and why I got your cell phone number instead of your office phone. He said, "Yes, someone mistakenly published my cell phone number on the internet as my office phone. Thank you for telling me it was on the internet because I was getting a lot of calls like yours and I couldn't figure out how my patients were getting my personal cell phone number. It is changed now," and we both laughed.

He asked, "So how is everything else going in your life?" I excitedly reported, "The flashbacks, body memories, nightmares, anxiety and panic attacks are gone." I explained that Sandy and I were working through a lot of my trauma issues and I don't have to take my sleeping pills to sleep anymore. We worked through the source of me feeling panicked and intimidated when conflict arises, and also the weight gain and loss back and forth issues. I also explained about the safety bag we developed and how I have learned to take care of myself by taking time out for myself. I am so happy now because I am not reverting back to a child unless we are in her office and making it happen with the EMDR and brainspotting therapy.

He said, "You have a great counselor to be doing so well! I am so proud of you, you are doing great! I think we can wait for three months before seeing you again because you are doing so well." I was so happy because I felt like my life was finally getting back on track. He said, "Well, I guess this is good-bye for three months then. Keep up the good work with your counselor." I told him I would and walked down the hallway with confidence that this was another milestone of reclaiming my life.

Chapter 19
Art and Attachment Therapy

I recognized the collage as full of symbols which were important to my life. The symbols reflected how I thought about my experiences and myself. In the collage I saw a chalk board with "Test Today" written on in. I felt that everyday God was testing me. He was giving me another cross to bear. Toilet Paper was a necessity that I didn't always have growing up so we had to use paper bags, or wash rags. I needed Advil PM sleeping pills to sleep because of nightmares. The bird cage with the door open represented my feelings and secrets trapped inside and now they were being released. A firefighter represented being saved from the house fire at the age of four years old.

Other symbols were important to understanding myself and my journey. There was a cookie in the collage that reminded me of grandma, Angelica. We used to cook, brownies and rice crispy bars. I had been happy then. The prize ribbon represents something worthwhile so I entered college and stayed for seven years and received four degrees. I needed to feel the accomplishment of walking down the aisle to accept my diplomas. I didn't know how to even find this good feeling until I started participating in the half marathons.

There was so much to understand about myself! A tree with the sunlight shining through light represented hope as it peaks through the branches which are the obstacles in life. The child with a bandage on his neck represented the several injuries I experienced from poor supervision. I never felt loved by my parents unless they were fighting to keep me alive. My injuries were often life threatening. A miner trapped in a cave symbolized my trapped feelings about my mother. She could be nice at times but when her alcoholism was out of control I can't be with her. This was very difficult for me, because I was so close to her. I couldn't forget the help she gave me while she was sober and I was struggling as a teenage mom. The miner in the collage made it out of the cave by pulling himself out of the huge black hole with a rope. This symbolizes the struggle I had coming out of the darkness and into the light as I tried to leave the negative memories behind me.

I wanted to remember positive memories from the past and noticed the ones yet to come. I lost a lot of years to trauma and grief and with the PTSD, conversion and somatization disorders. I missed the positives that were in my life, such as my children and husband. I was trying just to survive each day. I let my trauma take over my life. I kept remembering being home alone after witnessing my sister, Sonya, lying on the floor after overdosing. Then my parents disappeared with her and left Victoria and I at home as we anxiously waited to hear if our sister would live or die. I was 12 years old.

I realized that the lunch meat in the picture represented limited food because my mom would buy cigarettes and soda instead of food on the table. Sometimes we would go two or three days without eating, unless it was a school day and we had free hot lunch. I had the choice to go to Stella's house or starve but at her house I was sexually abused in exchange for food, which I did at the age of seven on.

Cindy responded with empathy and sadness for what I had been through. She also created a collage as I created mine. She shared with me what she saw when she listened to my struggles at each session so far.

The first item on Cindy's collage list was children playing on the sofa jumping which represents chaos in the house, children being loud, having fun and then disciplined when lamps break, as we tested our parents to see how wild we could get.

Fire, in Cindy's collage of her impressions of me, represented that I saw fires around me and felt that I needed to put them out in order to protect my family, whether it is danger from a family member or a perceived outside danger.

Then, there was a woman sitting on a sofa with her feet crossed with her legs resting on her chest, while holding a cup of tea. Nearby there is a table with the task of unfolded clothes waiting to be folded which represents me just needing some time for myself to relax and to take care of myself without chaos.

A woman in a life boat in a lake surrounded by hungry alligators represented my struggles. It was like I was in a lake of alligators and was dodging each one as I dealt with each memory one by one, with the symptoms of my anxiety disorders.

On the shore were people who represented all the people who were observing my struggles and how I coped with them. They were watching how I was still able to live each day working hard, receiving promotions, and taking care of my families' needs. Now I have added the hard work in therapy.

Cindy also read what she wrote on the back of the collage. "I am one who longs to be present in the moment with myself. I am one who wants to find what is authentic to me. I am one who travels thru chaos."

After she was done reading the statements, I told her I believed that all of the statements were true.

I was in awe that we only met a few times and Cindy could really understand me and my struggles. I felt so comfortable at this point to move on in therapy with no limitations on what I would share with her because I felt she was a very trust-worthy person.

We ended the session by putting my rock back in the bowl and answering that I would take home with me the feeling that I was a strong woman who could handle anything that came her way. I was a confident and accomplished woman. I was a loving person and will continue to be as I try to get through all my struggles while taking care of my family, facing each new challenge with a positive attitude that the new day brings.

Cindy retrieved me from the waiting room for our fifth session. I followed her with no energy and a half smile. She realized I was having a difficult day. When we sat down in the therapy room, she asked, "Are you feeling ok?" I told her it was a tough week. She then said, "Okay, today I will let you pick from my intention cards instead of picking a rock."

That seemed to cheer me up. I started to feel better as I looked through the cards. I told her it was hard to just choose one so she gave me permission to choose a few. I picked Letting Go, Strength and Hope. Cindy asked to explain my intentions: Letting Go is trying to let go of the relationship with my mom. I haven't seen her since the end of June and it was hard because I miss her and still loved her. This has been the longest time away from her and I hadn't communicated with her even on the phone.

The kids were giving me a hard time too because they miss their grandpa and wanted to see him. They keep saying, "Mom, he is dying and we don't know how much time he has left." I have no doubt they want to see him but I know they are also manipulating me because they want to play in the game room that their grandpa made for them in the basement. Strength was trying to stick to what I had said and that was when she stops drinking, we will see her.

The idea of Hope is the need to keep hope alive. I wanted to believe that everything will turn out okay. I will continue on my path of healing while my daughters and I struggled with the new boundary I had set with my parents. Some days I felt like I was losing the battle with overcoming my traumas. Despair happens when the symptoms get overwhelming and then I have the kids and everyday life problems.

I asked Cindy, "What will we do today for our project?" She replied, "I think another collage will do you good today because you seemed to enjoy it the last two sessions." Cindy put the soft music on while I started going through the magazine pages.

After I had enough pages, I started to cut out pictures without being sure of what the collage would look like but I was very excited by the images I found. When I was done cutting, I began to paste the images on the paper. When I was finished, I felt it was still missing something. I added inspiring words to it.

Since Cindy didn't give me any directions or limitations this time, I pulled a fast one and did another collage on the back side of the page. Cindy observed me as we both smiled, not saying a word. I felt so calm and happy now because I was creating something so beautiful that I could take home and reflect on it each day.

I didn't know what the images stood for when I chose them so the meanings would have to unfold as I talked to Cindy about them. There was a picture of a relaxing place with a hammock attached, hanging from two palm trees along with a pillow to rest my weary head. There are no people around which represented a safe and calm place that I could go in my mind to be alone and meditate while thinking positive thoughts. A sky of light pink and the dark blue water symbolized calmness, beauty and safety. The blue waters could be calm at times until the waves became dangerous. When it gets rough, it represents my struggles with memories and symptoms from anxiety disorders that I have to overcome each day. The rough waves can return to small ripples and steadiness returns with my positive and healing thoughts. The last symbol was a window with one side darkened and one clear side: my abusers and light side where I long to be.

A woman with her eyes closed in a meditative state of mind while the sun was shining on her face with a partial smile represented the need for me to find a quiet place to meditate and to take time out to care for myself. It showed the need to know I was worthy of a break from the kids, cooking, cleaning and other stresses of life. Also, I needed to learn to take a break from my trauma and accept that I have the right to command a peaceful uncluttered mind.

Water running from a faucet and filling a silver bowl represents God purifying me by washing and forgiving all my sins, as my mind, body and soul were healed. I also wrote statements on my collage on each part: The windows: Darkness, abusers are winning and have all the power. Light: silenced no longer, fight back.

I glued down a woman's face which represented me. Saw myself going through to the light.

The running water from the faucet meant I was pure in God's eyes. The pink sky represented hope and safety, enough to relax and enjoy life. The dark blue water represented strength, power, perseverance, forgiveness, love, embracing God and family, finding the positives and surrendering to the process.

Going up one palm tree were the words "Survivor" and from the same palm tree crossing over into the hammock I wrote, "Keep journaling and publish the book to create awareness."

Second collage was of a child running through the grass with a smile of achievement running away from my abusers who were blurry images I was barely able to see. I left them in the past as I run toward the future of happiness, safety, and the absence of sexual abuse and neglect. With the words Fun Fuel represents energy and how full of life I was.

A Mother lying down with her baby in a comforting state represents safety, love and care. The mother represents my adult self being the mother to the baby, my "child within", to help her move on from the darkness into the light of healing.

The green germ with a rain hat and coat with a frightened look on his face represented healing my conversion and somatization disorders. The green germ will be destroyed and will not exist once the healing process is complete. I will be returned to good health. I will have no more episodes of fainting, hives, **unexplainable** pain, high blood pressure, obesity, etc.

I also wrote statements on this collage: A child running through the grass. Put the abusers behind you and live freely.
Abusers blurred in the background—Powerless.
Fun Fuel—Find yourself. I used to have a lot of energy and was enthusiastic about life and somehow I lost myself, so I need to find her and continue living care free and happy.
Mother -You're loved
Baby -Leslie's rebirth
Green Germ- conversion and somatization disorder disappeared

When I was finished, I asked Cindy how she liked it, as I told her, "I know I didn't follow the rules by doing both sides." "You didn't give me that rule this time." We both laughed as she replied, "You're right I didn't. And I usually don't allow writing on the collages either but I could see you needed to and so I left you to create what you needed."

She further commented about my progress and that she was proud of all the hard work I have been doing because it is not easy to go through everything I am going through: work, raising a family, an ex-husband to contend with, and time for myself.

We went back to the other side of the room and sat on the sofa to end the session with what I will take with me today. I said, "Today was a great day. I came in upset, sad, defeated and I am going to leave with strength, confidence, restored energy, hope, continuing the process with gusto, and being kind to myself." Cindy was very pleased with my response as she told me to take care of myself.

I brought my binder to show Cindy my art work I did over the weekend that was very personal to me. As she opened the door she noticed the notebook, "You brought some things today." I proudly marched down the hall to the therapy room.

"I have things to share in my binder whenever you are ready during therapy today." She said, "That is great!" Cindy started out the session with having me pick a rock. I picked one with rough and sharp edges that symbolized a rough road with difficult decisions to make. I told her, "My intentions were to let go of things I cannot control and now it is time to ask for help by taking time for myself to exercise, eat healthy, reduce stress, take control of my life. My symptoms seemed to want to control me! I want to revitalize my relationship with my husband."

I told her of the decision to let my ex-husband have joint custody for six months, and then I would have them for six months. She looked a little confused, but asked, "How did you come to this decision?"

I told her I cried for two days when the papers were delivered to my house which stated Randy had filed for joint custody. I remembered everything he did to me, Sabrina and Veronica. I also told her what he had done in the past was the biggest thing that I had to let go because this had been the biggest stressor in my life constantly fearing for the worse and not letting Randy be a dad to the girls because of those memories. I told Cindy, "I am still afraid of what may happen with him and Veronica. She has a temper too but both girls say he doesn't have a temper anymore."

She asked, "Do you trust your decision?"

I told her that, "I have been living in the past and after a lot of reflection and a long talk with Randy, I needed to forgive him for the past and to give him a chance to be a good father to the girls. Otherwise, the resentment and hatred that the girls seem to have for me will strengthen and I may lose them when they are 18 years old. I figured this way if it doesn't work out then they will stop blaming me for the relationship issues they have with their dad. It is time to have them see how their dad is and for him to see how they are to me. It has been a hard road for me with my own issues but then you add in two teenagers who are fighting for more freedom. I watch them carefully and we get into power struggles."

Cindy was listening and looking kindly at me and I continued, "My life experiences have shaped me to always be cautious which doesn't give them much time with their friends. I keep them in public settings so they are never alone with people so the likelihood of sexual abuse is minimal. I do let them go on church trips and have those friends over and they get to go to their house once in a while. But, the school kids scare me for some reason. I don't trust them."

Cindy said, "Well maybe this will be a good change for you."

I told her, "I will be excited when I have time to exercise, lower my stress and to maybe strengthen my confidence by joining a women's self defense class at a martial arts place downtown. I am afraid of what may happen to the girls but know they are old enough to tell and to call the police, if needed. I have to let go of the control because I cannot control everything in my life. It is too exhausting. There is also a social worker, who will still be working with the girls until December because of their probation. I will also talk to the schools about the changes in our lives and ask them to report anything worrisome to the social worker."

Cindy said, "It sounds like you have a good plan in place now let's see what you brought to show me." I quickly reached for my binder and first showed her what I drew in the hospital:

1. I showed her my safe place of a picture waterfall which relaxes me when I am stressed out. I explained that I use positive imagery to calm myself down, which I learned in therapy with Sandy. I imagine that I am there with my feet in the water and my toes are gently touching the slimy rocks. I listen to birds and the water dripping while watching the small circles as I splash gently with the tips of my toes. There are statements such as cool water on my feet. I hear the water trickling down. It's a feeling of calmness and happiness. Additional imagery in the picture is at the bottom is the "child within" standing next to the adult me. My "child within" says, "I am starting to trust my adult self to take care of me. I am starting to feel loved and safe. I don't need to surface as much." My adult self says, "I work too hard for everyone and neglect myself. I want to take time to be the mom to my "child within". She needs my love and protection. There are flashes of feeling successful in my job when I receive praise from my boss. When I receive compliments and praise it's hard to accept it because I don't feel worthy."

2. The second item I showed her was the picture of a peacock I made with feathers and fake flowers on top of the page. I told her how drugged I was in the hospital and this felt soft, safe and calming to me.

3. I had another picture of me in the center and on it I wrote all of the characteristics I missed about myself such as confidence, intelligent, beautiful, organized, thinner, positive self-image, strength, happy, positive attitude, restored high energy, and living life to the fullest.

Then I went on to show her what I did over the weekend at home:

I did a collage with the intention of showing faith which I called *Learning from God*. It had angels, a rosary, a person who looked lost in a dessert, then words, Do not judge your neighbor until you walk a day in their shoes, along with the words A Personal Encounter, and, at the bottom of the page, a baby with the words: Use Your Voice For the Voiceless.

I also showed another collage of my sisters and I entitled: Soul Sisters—A Story of Joy and Sorrow. It had two photos of us: one as a group at a younger age and one of us recently when we ran half a marathon together. The pictures captions were Bonds of Affection and Cry for Help under the photo of the past. For the present photo The Painful Truth, a runner finds a physical outlet for emotional suffering. I also write Healing the Mind, Body and Spirit.

The last collage I showed Cindy was of me and the struggle I endured during the half marathon, over thirteen miles. I told her my life has been one big struggle and this half marathon seemed impossible but I did it. This was the turning point in my life which taught me that if I put my mind into something I can accomplish all of it. It is worth the fight to heal, forgive my abusers, let go of the hurt inside, to let go of control, and to help my "child within" merge into the confident adult I deserve to be.

Cindy said, "I am proud of you. Your collages are beautiful especially the one with your sisters. She then told me we don't have too much time left but wanted to talk about our next project." She said, "We have a choice between making a Native American prayer stick, wishing stick or a doll made out of nylon."

As Cindy was explaining the projects I was trying to be patient as I wanted to jump up and scream my choice. When it was my turn to talk,

I told her I choose the doll because I used to have a doll made of nylon named Meg that my sister, Andie, made for me when I was little. I used to tell her all my secrets that I couldn't tell anyone. I would cry and tell her all my hurts, joys and disappointments. Then one day what seemed to me the unthinkable happened. My sister's, Victoria, dog, Snuggles, ate Meg and all I could see around my bedroom was her stuffing, with her eyes looking at me from the floor. It almost destroyed me because I no longer had an outlet to let go of my emotions, and I lost a close friend. From that day forward, I stuffed my feelings.

Cindy said, "I think a doll is a great idea." She further explained what we would do at the end of the project. I told her I will make this doll as a symbol of my rebirth that holds hope, confidence and forgiveness. Cindy asked for my permission to read me the short book: *For Children Who were Broken* by Elia Wise. It was a very short book but I could identify with the content. We ended the session by putting my rock back in the bowl. Cindy gave me a hug. I could really feel us bonding as counselor and patient.

I first apologized at the next session for Veronica skipping her appointment. I told her she has decided not to come to counseling anymore and that I contacted her social worker because it was going against her court order. She said, "She is tired of people telling her how to live her life and people judging her artwork." I think this was coming from her dad because he didn't believe in therapy and now the girls were following him. I think he was worried about what they may remember about him and his sons. I decided to leave it up to the social worker to take care of the situation.

Then we started our session with setting my intentions. Today, my intention were to let go of the girls completely for a while and to focus on myself. Cindy asked, "How are you today?" I hated that question. I started to cry as the adult and the "child within" felt the hurt that occurred today after work just before I came to therapy. I explained I felt overwhelmed with hurt and the feeling of humiliation as I told her what happened:

Flashbacks in Post-Traumatic Stress Disorder: Surviving the Flood

The girls left their special shampoo and conditioner for their hair because I just bought them both hair highlights products. As I approached their dad's house, their cousin ran inside the house as I parked the car and started toward the door. As I was almost right in front of it, Uncle Ken, his friend Ben and his girlfriends came rushing out of the door, as the girls followed. It seemed very suspicious to me. With everyone surrounding me, I handed the bag with the shampoo and conditioner to Sabrina. She said to me in a loud cocky voice, "I don't need this. Dad got us shampoo and conditioner last night." She seemed pleased with herself as she disrespected me. Her uncle told her to keep it for next month.

I went to hand Veronica her clothes that she asked me to bring over after I washed them for her. As I handed the bag to her, she took the bag abruptly yanking it out of my hands. She said with a condescending voice, "Thanks, I guess." I tried to keep my head up to act like it didn't bother me. I tried to hug Sabrina and she gave me a half hug but Veronica pushed me away and said, "I don't want a hug from you." They both dismissed me like I was a piece of dirt.

I turned around with my back towards them and walked away with my son's hand in mine. I started to cry as my four year old said, "I don't like Sabrina and Veronica. They make you cry." I told him everything will be okay.

Cindy said, "I am so sorry you went through that as she explained that they are just continuing to trigger my "child within." I sobbed as I told her, "I know that but it really hurts and it is hard not to take what they did personally after I have been taking care of them for their entire life. Their dad did nothing. So many of the times he cancelled, I tried to make up for their disappointment of him. I know now that my ex-husband hasn't changed and my daughters are choosing to take the abuser's way instead of the healing non-abuser way."

I told Cindy what Sandy told me that maybe it is time to separate from them for awhile and only focus on myself. Cindy agreed. After we discussed it a little further I was able to calm down.

The time for our session was almost up so we decided to start a collage focusing on what babies' needs are. I started to rip out certain magazine pages that spoke to my "child within" in some way. Cindy said "After we do the collage and discuss the letter you wrote as the "child within", we will start to make the nylon doll."

I was looking forward to the doll project the most. We ended our session with what I was taking with me. I told her that I was confident that healing will happen and that I can let go of the girls so I can become a healthier, better mom, when they return in six months. While walking to the van, I felt strong and happy. I felt supported by both of my counselors and I trusted in their advice.

The next time, I went into art therapy feeling confident, strong, and happy. For this session, Cindy had me pick cards to set my intentions. I picked Confident, Strong, Stabilized and Self Awareness. I told Cindy, "I feel strong and confident that I can continue each day on my healing journey. I feel stabilized and aware of my emotions and the fact I can keep everything under control."

Cindy said, "Did you bring your letter from your "child within?" Before I have you read it, I want you to finish your collage." So we went into the art therapy room to finish the collage, while listening to soft, calming music. When I was finished, we went back into the sitting area of the room to discuss the collage.

- There was a picture of a child with a map trying to navigate through the woods with several different signs from which to choose. I felt it represented me because I had to navigate by myself making some wrong turns, facing danger and ultimately finding the correct path.

• There were pictures of babies' needs that were necessities such as diapers, cereal, juice, carrots and cheese which I felt represented what I needed but didn't always get from my parents.

• Necessities like boots, hats, and mittens were not always obtained by my parents. Usually family members would see we didn't have them and they would buy them or someone else would because they saw us cold in the snowy weather.

• I put a baby in a car seat on the collage because this represented the need for safety in the car which I don't remember feeling because of the car exhaust and my mother telling us not to fall asleep. Also, my dad drove off the road when he would zone out or fall asleep and my mother would yell, "Wake up!"

• The baby in a picture frame had the words "Is this what I looked like?" My parents didn't have any photos of me when I was a baby so I always felt like I didn't belong in my family. When my sisters would get mad at me, they would tell me that I was adopted and that they weren't my real sisters which reinforced the lonely feeling I was already internalizing.

• Books were something I don't remember as a child. No one read to me and tucked me in at night.

• There is a picture of a little baby playing by herself. This represents the feeling of being alone and having to entertain myself. There is a picture of a boy with doctor toys playing with his mother. I don't remember my mother ever playing with me.

• A clock with Tweetie bird is on my collage because I felt like time was running out when I was a young teenager. At the age of 18 years old I felt like I needed to have a family right away because I felt so old inside.

• There is a photo of a girl all in pink, even her hair. This represents fantasy because we didn't have a lot of toys so my sisters and I would have to think up our own games. I remember my sisters and me dancing to music and having concerts for my grandparents.

• There was a photo with a child laughing with her father while eating together. I don't remember sitting down and eating as a family very often.

I then read my letter from the "child within" out loud:

Dear God:
Please help me! Why can't you hear me? I cry every night that my belly is empty. Why doesn't anyone feed me? I tell my mommy that I am hungry. She yells at me. She tells me she fed me but I don't remember eating. I rush to the refrigerator to find a jar of mayo then find the cupboard is empty. I feel confused. If I was fed where is all the food? Why does my belly feel sick and empty? Doesn't my mommy want to feed me? Was I a bad girl?

I have to find food on my own: I go to my Grandmother Angelica's house and my Great Uncle Charlie gives me long bad good-byes. My face hurts, I feel dirty and confused inside. I go to my friend's, Stella, house and find food but am expected to do bad things to her brother, Frank, or see Stella's dad hurt her. God, are you punishing me for what I have to do? Please forgive me? I need food. My mommy needs her money for her beer and cigarettes so I have to do the things I do.

I get injured and no one is there to protect me from getting hurt on the barbwire fence, a rock hitting me over the head, almost drowning and almost burned to death in the house fire. Where is everyone? Is anyone out there? Why does my *grandmother, Maggie, hate me? She shoves food down my throat causing me to choke. I feel like I can't breathe. I tell her I am sorry but I am full but she says I have to eat all that is on my plate or she will make me. My sisters try to protect me by hitting and jumping on her but she is too strong.*

Why do my parents make me say good-bye to my Great Uncle Charlie? Don't they see what he does to me? Don't they care? Was I bad and that is why they make me? I walk throughout the town by myself and no one is around. Where is everyone? I can't find my sisters, my mommy or daddy, I am scared. Where did everyone go? I feel like everyone left me behind.

Why did my mommy let my uncle and aunt drive me to a basketball game while my uncle and aunt smoked pot and drank beer? I couldn't breathe with all the windows shut. I tried to get on the floor of the car and that helped a little. I felt scared and unsafe as I heard the car slide into the gravel a few times and the loud laughter scared me.

Why did my mom let us swim on the side of the road after it rained? A car almost hit us and it scared me. Why did my mom think it is okay to get our swim suits on in the middle of a rain and lightning storm? Didn't she know it wasn't safe? Where is my daddy?

I feel cold as I try to keep warm as I walk to get to the bus for school. My mommy and daddy can't afford mittens and a hat for me. My feet are cold because I don't have boots. I am thankful to have a jacket that my mommy had from when my sister, Victoria, was my age.

Why does my daddy get really mad and hit us with a leather paddle. Doesn't he love me? Why does he want to hurt me? My butt is red and sometimes he leaves welts but I don't think he meant it. He was just really angry with me. Why does my mommy yell and drink a lot? Doesn't she love me? I need hugs, kisses and love but her beer and cigarettes are too important to her.

My mommy and daddy fight a lot when he goes to work at night with his guitar. When will they stop fighting? I try to cover my ears with my pillow but I can still hear them yelling. My grandmother, Angelica, gives me love, cookies, brownies, and food. Why can't my mommy and daddy be like grandma? They don't even have time to play with me. I either play with my sisters or by myself.

Why does my daddy want to scare me? The doggy in the window and the blood sucker incidents scared me. I feel scared, panicky and unsafe. God, can you tell my daddy to stop hurting me and scaring me? He'll listen to you.

My sisters are supposed to watch me but they run too fast with their friends and I am left behind alone. I am scared. Where did they go? How do I get back home?

Why do my sisters and I have to go to the bar with mom? I watch my sisters' dance with the men there as mom watches, laughs, and drinks her beers?

Why did my sisters scare me by leaving me behind when they broke into the school to play basketball? It was dark and I couldn't see. I was thankful when they came back to get me out of there.

I feel like no one loves me because people hurt me. Where are my mommy and daddy to protect me? I know you are busy but God please help my mommy and daddy be better to me. God, I know I am asking a lot but I need help, I am only a little girl.

Love Tweetie

My art therapist thanked the "child within" for sharing her letter and reassured her that she will get her needs met from now on. I told the "child within," "I love you and will make sure all your needs are met: the need for food, protection, love, clothing, and security. I promise you will never be left alone and no one will ever hurt you again!" I could feel how relieved, happy and loved the "child within" felt. I left therapy feeling confident and free that once again the silence was released and secrets were revealed.

At our next session, we did attachment therapy to help further integrate the adult and "child within." Cindy took me through guided imagery and told me to imagine myself on a swing as the adult. She told me that someone was coming towards me and she would take me on a journey. I pictured me as a child coming closer and closer until she reached me. I stopped swinging as she reached out for my hand. She wanted to share her special time going to the candy store. We both were holding hands as we walked to the store talking about what we would buy. After we collected our candy, my child self told me she wanted to take me to a special place. We went to her secret hiding place where Great Uncle Charlie couldn't go because he was too old to climb on the rocks.

We sat there together eating candy. Cindy told my adult self to tell my "child within" something to comfort her about what happened with Great Uncle Charlie. My adult self looked at her "child within" and said, "Sweetie, you know that it wasn't your fault what Great Uncle Charlie did to you. The adults in your life should have stopped him from hurting you. I am here now and I will protect and love you. I won't let anyone hurt you again." My adult self hugged the "child within" tightly as I imaged her saying, "Thank you. I need someone to love and protect me."

The next session was the tenth session and it was even more powerful than the other sessions because again we did attachment therapy with guided imagery. I was able to go deeper into my issues and feel what I had been through. Cindy started out by telling me that we are by a lake and we were going to go somewhere special. There were people expecting me. She told me that I was really light so I was able to walk on top of the water. On the other side was a forest. As I walked through the forest, I cleared the branches from in front of me until I reached a clearing in the forest. There was a fire there and Cindy told me to sit down and get comfortable with my surroundings. She told me there will be three people visiting me tonight: my wise woman, power woman, and my fear woman. Each will bring a gift.

Cindy asked me to imagine what a wise woman would look like. I thought of my grandmother, Angelica, and how she was my role model growing up. She seemed to know all the answers. My wise woman did resemble my grandmother as she walked out to meet me. I asked her to sit in front of me on the other side of the fire. She had long flowing white hair, a kind smile, and was wearing a beautiful dress that had beadwork and was several colors. Her gift to me was a beautiful beaded purse with a moon on it.

Then Cindy asked me to imagine what my power woman would look like. What characteristics would make my power woman strong enough to survive everything I have been through? I thought of God's love and forgiveness of all my sins. Then I imagined my big heart and the gift of forgiveness. Then I see a small shadow as my power self arrived. It was my three year old self. She had a smile on her face and brought a lot of energy to the atmosphere. Her gift to me was her warm and loving embrace, along with a heart made of strong ceramic. I asked her to sit on the right side of the wise women on the other side of the fire. She was my power woman because it takes a lot for her to be able to keep loving, smiling, and accepting others with an open heart even though she suffered so much. I loved her and felt her strength.

Cindy asked me to think of what I feared the most. Who do I fear to see and face? I imagined myself between the ages of 14-18 years old. That is when I needed help the most. I felt overwhelming fear as the image of me at fourteen seemed to arrived unexpectedly from the opposite direction that the others have come. She had on heavy makeup, was wearing tight jeans and a blue shirt. She felt unaccepted, alone, scared and empty inside. She had no gift to offer me as she stood embarrassed and ashamed.

She felt judged, disappointed and disgusted at herself as she looked at the wise woman.

I gave her a hug and told her the gift she offered me was her courage and strength to come knowing that she may not be accepted by all who were there. I asked her to sit on the right side of me. I accepted her and loved her and needed her to feel it. I wanted her to know those hard days were over and it was never her fault that she thought so little of herself that her actions reflected it. Whatever she had done, she had done from pain and low esteem. I was sorry it all happened that way but those abusive days were over now.

Cindy then told me to remember these women and when I need to draw on their strength to do so in my times of need. We sat still for a few minutes as I meditated on all their strengths and individual gifts. Cindy asked me to slowly come back into the room and when I was ready I opened my eyes.

Cindy and I discussed this empowering and positive experience. I felt my own strength as I left the session and walked back into the world as I knew it with the struggles of PTSD, conversion and somatization disorders. I had a feeling of renewal and strength as I take on the attitude that I could accomplish and cope with anything that came my way.

Chapter 20
Complete Resolution

Rape Surfaces Again!

The entire week I have been unsettled by a white car that is parked in the school parking lot next to my house. The car is in a parking stall facing my home and has been there for several weeks. There has been no one around the car. I felt scared that someone was watching me.

I saw the Sheriff parked by the white car. He was against the fence facing the car as I walked up to the side of his car. I explained that another Sheriff told me to report anything suspicious because this summer the school was broken into. So I continued to tell him how concerned I was because the white car was there for several weeks. He told me he ran the plates and it wasn't stolen but the strange thing is it has official plates on it.

He continued to tell me that even if the officer lived in the area and just parked there that he wouldn't be authorized to put an official plate on the car. He told me he would check into it because he was on duty for the next four days. The car is still there and no one got back to me on my concern.

I left the house this morning and the car was still there. On the way to therapy, I think disturbing thoughts; the worse the thoughts, the faster I drove to get to therapy. When I reached my therapist office and sat down, I told Sandy that I am paranoid about the car. I think Bret and Officer Jon are going to attack me or kidnap my daughters. She told me that I wasn't paranoid. She explained that the little girl is scared because she wasn't protected by her parents so she is being triggered. These triggers keep occurring because the little girl never felt safe as a child and was never taught how to keep herself safe.

I continued to tell Sandy that I felt Officer Jon and Bret were watching me. Officer Jon was the high school liaison officer when I got hit by the car that I felt Bret set up. When the attendance lady told Officer Jon what Bret said to other students in the lunch room about my accident, Bret said, "They didn't do the job right. She should have been killed." Officer Jon replied "People say things they don't mean every day." Since nothing was investigated, I was convinced that Officer Jon was involved in the accident because he used to be buddy buddy with Bret in the lunch room. I was terrified each night that Officer Jon and Bret were waiting for the right time to hurt me or take my daughters and rape them like Bret did to me. Sandy reassured me that I am no longer in danger because I am an adult and have resources to protect myself.

Sandy asked if I wanted to work on releasing the trauma associated with the triggers. I nodded so we proceeded to get me settled on the sofa and notice the relaxed parts of my body and the tense part, which was my upper chest. Concentrating on the relaxed parts of my body, we created a grid. My grid was first feet connected to hands, then to elbows, shoulders, ears and mouth. The feet, eyes, ears and mouth were the release points. We then established the brain spot while using the pointer. This allows me to have a focal point where I can visualize God holding the little girl in his arms while looking into her eyes taking all the pain away and healing her. Sandy asked, "How old are you?" I replied, "14 years old." Sandy told me to breathe in through my nose, release through my mouth and just feel the grid, as she verbally retraced the grid. I visualized it and settled in.

I told her my heart was broken and hurt because I trusted him. He made me feel special and told me he loved me. Then he isolated me from all my friends until I had none. Sandy told me that is what deviants do.

She told me to visualize God placing his hand on my heart to heal it. She asked, "What are you feeling." I told her I need to cry. I could feel my cheeks and throat were getting tight. Sandy told me to cry it out because it needs to be released from my body. As I visualized what happened to me, I could feel the tears starting to come down my right cheek, then my left, as I voiced how I felt: "He had no right to take my innocence away, rape me and make me feel fear, and stalked me for four years.

I relived how he drove me home and left me at my parent's driveway when he reminded me, "If you tell anyone I will kill you." His words echoed in my ears. Sandy affirmed that I was doing great and to keep releasing the feelings and keep seeing God holding me in his arms. Sandy reminded me that these feelings have been stuck inside for 21 years and need to be released and that is what will heal my mind, body and spirit. The reason this is happening right now is because your body feels you can release it now because you are in a safe relationship with your husband. She reminded me if I need to take a break we can stop at anytime. I told her no, I need to go through the entire thing.

A few minutes went by and again she asked, "What are you feeling or seeing?" "I am looking at the front door of my parent's house and am scared to go in. I went through the entire situation by myself and didn't want to witness it again." Just then I felt God's hand on my shoulder as he told me to trust him. He led me into my house and upstairs to my bedroom. This time instead of me hugging my stuffed animals for comfort, I saw God holding me in his arms. He told me he was sorry this happened to me. That he would help to take care of me. I asked for forgiveness for having sex so young. He put his hand on my head and forgave me because I am his child. I then saw myself walking down the stairs step-by-step by-step trying to be quiet so I could go take a bath unnoticed. Tears are rolling down my face and my legs are shaking. Sandy asked, "Are you still okay, Leslie?" I nodded yes. She asked, "What do you see or feel?"

I told her my heart feels better but now I feel like I am going to vomit. She quietly and gently placed the garbage can next to me as she explained that my body is trying to release the stored feelings. She asked if there were a color associated with the feelings. I told her white because of the toilet color. I explained that I was vomiting in my bathroom after I got home from being raped. Again, I felt God was there with me. When I was finished vomiting, I heard the water running. I sat on the toilet and look in the mirror to see why I was hurting. God was there to comfort me as he helped me to stand up to go into the bath. I looked into God's eyes and he said, "This time it will not hurt. I will heal you." I stepped into the bath and cleaned my soiled body with Bret's scent trying not to think about each step of the rape and his house layout.

When I was finished, I felt better and God was there. He wrapped me in a white towel and told me I was pure again. He put me in a white night gown as he took me back upstairs and tucked me into bed. He told me that he will always be here for me and not to lose faith. I told him I was sorry for not seeing him before but I was so young and felt all alone. I used to think God was punishing me for my life choices but now I know that is not true. God kissed me on my head like a father would do and then he disappeared. I felt God's love and forgiveness.

Before the session ended, Sandy said, "We will do some earth mediation." She told me to close my eyes and visualize my feet in the ground and suck in the soil up my right leg down my left leg while breathing in and out releasing any stress that was left in my body. This process was repeated with each layer of the soil, rocks, etc. After we were all done, I felt so relaxed and a feeling of hope was in my heart. As we were walking back to the lobby, I told Sandy my cheeks felt numb, my legs felt tired, and my buttocks felt like they were quivering. She told me that my body is still releasing all the stress and warned me that I may be tired. She reminded me after doing so much that it is important to listen to my body and sleep.

Sandy Gives me a gift.

Sandy quietly was going through cards as I relaxed. She pulled out three cards and told me these are positive affirmation cards. She had me read them out loud:

1. My life works beautifully.
2. Everything in my life works, now and forevermore.
3. My healing is already in process.
4. My willingness to forgive begins my healing process. I allow the love from my own heart to wash through me, cleansing and healing every part of my body I know I am worth healing.
5. I am free to think wonderful thoughts. I move beyond past limitations into freedom. I am now becoming all that I am created to be.
6. Freedom is my divine right.

They all had positive images but the last one was my favorite because it had a picture of paper, an envelope, pen, a lit candle, ink refill for pen, a statue of a person's head, and a book. This symbolized to me exactly what I was doing and what my goals were. The card to me meant a person is burning the midnight oil while writing a book. The goal was for divine freedom I seek and to help others understand mental illness. These cards were a gift that I would cherish forever. I am confident that this will be the turning point of therapy, me changing myself to be healthier and to start caring for myself. I had to realize that everyone is old enough to take care of themselves. Now it is time for me to fight back with all my might to resolve all my demons, traumas, and emotional attachments to those traumas.

I felt so much gratitude to Sandy that I gave her a hug and thanked her for the tremendous gift of sight and a renewal of life and positive energy. I really felt hope that healing is possible, that I deserved to be healthy and without emotional issues.

The Use of EMDR

Sandy explained, "The memories will still be there but our objective with EMDR is to take the memories from the right side of your brain, where it holds the emotions of your trauma, which is stirring up emotions in the present, and to reprocess the memories to the left side where there is logic. Logic will tell you it happened in the past and not in the present." "After we can heal those memories, you will no longer be bothered by them because you will be able to recognize that it happened in the past." I replied, "That is what I want."

Sandy gave me the headphones to put on as she explained we will only do the EMDR today. I was excited to get started. Sandy laughed, "Leslie, you got one of the headpieces the wrong way." "You won't be able to hear too well." I fix it and laughed, "I guess I am too excited to start healing."

Sandy said we will start by making a grid okay. "Find the most relaxed part of your body. I replied, "My feet." Sandy, "Okay notice your feet and pick another spot." I replied, "My left cheek." Sandy, "Okay draw a line from your feet to your left cheek and notice that then find another spot." I replied, "My forehead" Sandy, "Okay draw a line from your feet to your left cheek and to your forehead and notice how that feels and pick another spot." I replied, "My right ear." Sandy, "Okay draw the line from your forehead to your right ear and notice how that feels." She explained, "This will be an exit spot where you will release all the emotions you have while we work today. Find another spot. I replied, "My right thigh." Sandy, "Okay draw a line from right ear to your right thigh and notice how that feels and pick one more spot. I replied, "My left shoulder." Sandy, "Okay draw a line from your right thigh to your left shoulder. "Now I am going to retrace your grid while you concentrate on it." "Draw a line from your feet to your left cheek, then to your forehead then to your right ear to your right thigh to your left shoulder and back to your feet. Take a moment to notice how that feels while strengthening the grid." Sandy asked, "Do you want the grid open or closed for this session." I replied, "Open."

Sandy took the pointer and told me to find the place that feels the most calm as she moved it from side to side. I found my brain spot to the left and up a little. This is the part of the brain that held the memories that we will be working on today.

Sandy, "I want you to imagine how bad it hurt when your daughters treated you with disrespect a few days ago at their dad's house." As I took my memory back to the incident I was sad again. Sandy asked, "What are you feeling?" I replied, "I am intimidated and feel discarded." Sandy asked, "When in your life have you felt this way?" "How old are you?"

I replied, "Three years old." The memory of the house fire resurfaced. I explained, "My uncle Nead is a very scary man who likes to intimidate, and have control over us and the situation." "After the fire, my uncle Nead took me and my sister, Victoria, upstairs where the fire happened. He screamed, while my mother was present, saying "Look at what you did!" My mother said and did nothing to protect us. I am feeling bad and intimidated as I look around and see only the framing of the walls left and everything is black and still smoldering. I see small amounts of smoke in the air. I felt like no one cared that my sister, Victoria, and I were okay. He continued yelling. "Your parents are renting this house." I continued to look around the room and still my mother is watching him yell at us with no response. I felt unprotected and terrified of what was going to happen to us.

Sandy said, "Okay now take that three years old little girl and comfort her with your adult self. Tell her that she is safe and that you will not let anyone hurt her anymore. Tell her it is not her fault that her mother left her unsupervised while she played with the matches. She is not to blame. Her mother should have been watching her. Reassure her that memory is in the past and that she can move on without being scared of her Uncle Nead because you will protect her."

I imagined myself scooping up the little girl who was terrified and crying and comforting her while I told my uncle to "Stop it! She is only a little girl. She doesn't understand what she did wrong! If you want to yell at someone go find her mother who should have been watching her." Both of us feel powerful and happiness as he retreats downstairs. I gently tell her as we look around the rooms, "When we play with matches this can happen." "If you ever find matches again it is really important that you give them to your mom or an adult and not to play with them, okay?" She agrees by hugging me tightly, not wanting to let go.

EMDR Only-Fire Healing

It was a great week and I was looking forward to going to therapy because I was ready to do more work to heal. Sandy greeted me with her smile, and asked, "How are you doing today?" I was so happy because I could reply, "Very good and you!" We got comfortable as Sandy retrieved my file. She said, "What are we working on today?" Then, "How do you feel when I bring up the house fire and your uncle yelling at you?" "On a scale 1-10 how much does it bother you?" I replied, "A five." She replied, "That is not good enough. We want it to be a zero where there are no fearful feelings or response in your body." "What do you feel when you are that three year old little girl?" I replied, "I feel that it was my fault." She asked, "What would you like to believe and feel?" I replied, "That it wasn't my fault and that my mom should have been watching me." Sandy made the statements stronger by saying, "So we want it to be, It wasn't my fault and that children need to be supervised." Then she explained that we are going to do EMDR only today. It would be different because during the session she will have me concentrate on the memory, while breathing in and out. Then she will stop and check in every so often to see what I am feeling in my body. I said, "Okay," but I didn't know what was in store for me, so I was a little scared.

She handed me the headsets and she told me to concentrate on the smoldering, black wall and the feelings of fear and intimidation. As she started the EMDR, I could feel my body starting to feel different as she let me concentrate for a while on the image and feelings but then she stopped the EMDR and said, "How are you doing?" "What are you noticing?" I told her, "My body is tense and my chest is tight and I feel terrified." She said, "Okay, now remember this is what the little three year old felt like," and reminded me that I was okay in the present. She continued with the EMDR machine for a few more minutes and stopped again. "Okay now what do you feel?" I told her, "My fear is still there but now my hands are tingly and my face is also tingly." "Leslie, now I want you to imagine your uncle yelling at you," as she turned the EMDR on again.

Then a few minutes went by as I concentrated on my uncle intimidating me while yelling and telling me, "Look at what you have done," while pointing to the black smoldering framing that used to be the wall. I tried to keep breathing in and out but it was hard to as I told Sandy, "It is getting hard to breathe and I am scared. I feel like I am breathing very shallow and it is really difficult." In a gentle voice Sandy told me to just keep breathing in and out, slow and calm."

I became very fearful of him and I felt unsafe to be by him. Sandy reminded me to bring in the adult me to comfort and help me process the memory. I imagined my adult self, yelling back at him telling him, "You don't talk that way to her. She is only a little girl who doesn't understand why you are yelling at her. If you want her to understand what she did wrong, you need to be calm and talk to her about the dangers of what she did." My breathing was getting too fast so Sandy reminded me to slow down. I imagined my adult self giving my "child within" the opportunity to tell him how I felt as I yelled at him, "It wasn't my fault my mommy should have been watching me." I pictured him being shocked and stunned as he retreated downstairs, as I felt powerful. After all these years, I took my power back from him.

I imagined my adult self kneeling down to my child's level and explaining gently, "When you play with matches this is what can happen. If you find matches you need to give them to your mommy, okay." After talking to the little girl, my adult self gave her a hug with her head resting on my shoulder.

She stopped the EMDR again and asks, "What are you noticing in your body?" I told her that my face was tingly radiating up toward my ears and that my hands were tingly. Sandy said, "What else?" I told her "I feel like something is floating in my stomach but I don't know what it is." She told me to concentrate on it and ask your body to reveal what it is" as she turned the EMDR back on. While still concentrating on the imagery of my uncle yelling and the black walls, I also concentrated on this object moving in my stomach for a few minutes. Then again the EMDR was stopped while Sandy asked, "What do you notice about that object now?" I told her, "I am not sure what it is." "Okay, ask your body if we should keep concentrating on it or if we should move on without it." The first thought that came to my mind was to go on without it.

So we did. The EMDR was turned back on as I kept on concentrating on the same spot but this time it felt as if a small peach pit was floating in my belly and as I breathed in it got larger. As I breathed out it became smaller. It was a strange sensation in my stomach. I felt tingly all over my body. As I concentrated on it more, it felt like it floated up to the top of my belly. Sandy stopped the EMDR and asks, "What are you noticing now?" I told her and she said, "Okay, let's go with it and keep going."

She noticed my breathing was getting too fast. She reminded me, "breathe in and out very slow and controlled." She stopped the EMDR again. I told her, "I feel like there is pressure in my stomach and the pit needs to come out because it is the fear, I think. My uncle scared me so bad that it went to the pit of my stomach." "I feel like I have the urge to vomit to get it out." Sandy said, "You can visualize yourself throwing up, you don't have to actually do it," as she moved the trash can near me just in case. "Okay let's visualize the pit coming up and out of your body." She started the EMDR again. I keep concentrating on the pit and the pressure as it moved up my stomach into my throat where it got caught. My entire body was tingly and pulsating. I communicated this to Sandy as she reassured me, "It's good. It means your body is releasing all the feelings you kept bottled up for all these years. These are just body memories."

Sandy suggested opening my mouth wide as I breathed out. I tried it and the pit started to move out of my throat toward the opening of my mouth but then disappeared and then I felt it in my nose. I started to laugh as I told Sandy "It is on the point of my nose but still inside." She said, "Okay there is a tissue box beside you. Let's try as you breathe out to blow your nose and I did it a few times and it was out." I felt a feeling of relief and a calm feeling come over me." It felt like a huge load was lifted off my shoulders.

She asked me, "Now how do you feel when I bring up the house fire and your uncle yelling at you. How true do the following statements feel?" "The fire was my fault?" I replied, "It feels false." Then she continued, "That children need to be supervised." I told her, "It felt true." "That the fire wasn't your fault; you were just a little girl." I replied again, "It feels true." I was overjoyed because logically as an adult I knew the fire wasn't my fault but the feelings inside communicated that it was my fault because the little girl still felt it.

Sandy took the headsets off and she told me, "This is how it feels to totally reprocess a memory. The memory gets successfully over to the left side of your brain where there is logic letting you know that the event happened in the past and that the fire wasn't your fault. Now your mind, body and the little girl believes it to be true."

I told Sandy that finally I understand why I would feel the pain above my belly button and then the pressure would come and I would vomit.

It was part of my conversion disorder. My body was remembering this trauma and my body was trying to release it. It felt empowering to know that the struggle with my health had a logical reason for occurring and that it wasn't all in my head as the doctor's probably thought.

Barbewire Fence EMDR

Right after that memory the little three year old girl took me to another memory of the barbwire fence. She shows me as I explain it to Sandy. "I am outside with my two sisters, Victoria and Sonya; we are playing hide and go seek. My glasses are off because I broke them. I am walking around and thought I saw them so I started to run toward the barbwire fence but I stop and think I went under it as I continued to run. All of a sudden I am stopped by the barbwire fence as I bang into it and am flung backwards on my back. I get up and start to run as I feel my hands and arms down beside my legs as they are swishing up and down to make me run faster to the house. I screamed, "Help me!" When I enter the doorway of the living room, I see my mom with her friend as I scream "Help me mommy!" She is in a panic as she gets a towel to try and stop the bleeding as she calls my grandmother who was making pies with my older sister, Andie. My grandmother rushes over to my house to take us to the hospital which was about 30 minutes away.

While I am lying in the car on my mother's lap I remember the towel having ice in it while my mom kept removing it and screaming the blood won't stop it is too much!" My mother yells for my grandmother to drive faster. My mom looks down at me and yells to not close my mouth because the right side of my tongue was almost severed, it was just hanging there. I start to feel sleepy and weak as she yells for me not to fall asleep because I may not wake up.

We finally get to the hospital as the doctors' rush me into the operating room to stitch my face. I remember my face not being frozen before the stitches because of the amount of blood I lost. There were many sets of hands stitching my face as I try not to cry because I am the brave one in my family. Afterwards the doctors gave me stickers and my grandmother took me out for malt. I remember feeling loved by my mother because of the concern she had for me when I was hurt.

Sandy said, "Okay can you comfort that little girl and tell her that she is safe. You are there to protect her and watch over her." As Sandy said this to me, I imagined the adult me arriving at the hospital and asking, "Where is the little girl that was just brought in?" I see her mother in the waiting room as I barge in and yell "Why can't you just watch and protect her?" "Wake up or the next time she may not make it!" As the doctors are stitching her tiny face, I quietly go into the room to hold her hand. I softly rub her hand and tell her, "Everything is okay. It will only take a little longer." She tells me it hurts and I respond with compassion, "I know it hurts honey but we need to do this. I will bring you to get a malt after we are all done!"

When it is all over, I imagined I take her in my arms and hug her telling her, "You are safe." "I am here now and nothing like this will ever happen again." She responds by hugging me tightly while sobbing telling me what happened and how scared she was because her mother was screaming at her in the car.

I thanked Sandy for helping me and told her, "I am really looking forward to going through this more and more to release all the memories I have." I left her office feeling empowered and free.

Part Eight
How I Survived the Flood

Chapter 21
Life After the Flood

Life after the flood is not easy. It is an ongoing process that you will do the rest of your life. However, it is easier than where you started. You get educated about your disorders, learn coping skills, and you get your life back or you create a new one that is full of new beginnings. I learned so much by getting help for my PTSD, conversion and somatization disorders. I can identify my triggers and calm the "child within" before my emotions or actions get out of control i.e. panic attacks and feeling an overwhelming fear and the need to flee. I can also recognize a trigger and use coping skills before it interrupts family activities.

Warning Signs of Abuse—It is important to know the warning signs of abuse. You were an abuse victim which includes:
- depression
- negative attitudes
- no positives reinforcement
- zoning out to get away from problems
- isolating yourself from family and friends
- dissociating
- poor hygiene
- angry outbursts
- being defensive
- crying spells
- numbing out, anxiety
- paranoia thinking people are out to hurt you
- reoccurring or unexplained illnesses
- being afraid to be alone, hating yourself
- hurting self

- suicide attempts
- a feeling of worthlessness
- not feeling safe
- need to be in control all the time
- overachiever
- overprotective of your children to the extreme
- hyper alert of surroundings
- reverting back to a child
- emotionally out of control
- sensitivity to sounds, smells and touch
- in fight or flight mode all the time waiting for the next threat to appear
- repeating childhood abuses with your children

Seek Professional Help—You need to find a therapist, counselor, and/or psychiatrist you can trust and with whom you make a connection. You may also need medications and admission into a hospital to help regulate the medication. It is okay if it takes a few tries before you find the right fit. Without this connection, you will not heal because you will not trust to be honest and open. You also need to trust the therapies that they suggest to you in order to heal. I am so lucky to have found the perfect fit with Sandy. She knows exactly what I need and when. She knows when to do trauma work or when to do resource building to allow myself to get stronger before continuing trauma work.

My art therapist was also a good fit because she is talkative like me. She taught me how to be creative and use artwork to express myself and to release my child emotions. It didn't matter if I was good at art. She encouraged me to express myself and have fun playing with the different art projects.

My psychiatrist was a great match too because he was able to diagnose me correctly just by listening to my life story. He was able to regulate my medication quickly after my hospital stay and maintains it so I stay on the path to healing with a healthy mind. These three people have forever changed my life and I am able to live a normal life because of their expertise.

Breaking the Silence and Telling the Secrets—This is a very hard step but it is the first step to healing. You give your abusers all the power over your mind, body and spirit by keeping their secrets and being silent. You need to regain your mind, body and spirit and send a clear message to the abusers that you are taking back your personal power.

The "child within"—You will need to learn how to connect with the "child within" to know what he or she needs to heal. It may be comfort from the bad people in your imagination, learning how to trust your adult self or other people, or learning how to play again. This is an important part of healing because without it you will not heal. Unresolved issues are where your triggers originate. Your therapist will help you uncover what the "child within" needs. This step is also about learning to take care of yourself before you can take care of others.

Find Support System—You need to find people who are going to help and support you through your healing process. It may be a support group, therapist, psychiatrist, a fellow survivor, friends, family, a coworker you can trust, or a pastor, etc. It is imperative to your healing success to rid yourself of toxic relationships. If it is your family, that is difficult. However, you will have to distance yourself until you are able to heal enough to recognize their unhealthy patterns and learn how to cope while in their presence. I had to do this with my parents. It was hard especially because I was so dependent on their acceptance, stuck in the good girl role and because I didn't know anything different, so their unhealthy lifestyle was normal to me.

I was so lucky to have a loving husband that had a lot of patience, understanding, and took a lot of the responsibilities that I couldn't do while I was sick. He had to be the mom and dad for a short time, plus he had an extra person to worry about. He loves me unconditionally which I never experienced before because all I knew all my life was abuse. Because I finally found a healthy relationship, it was safe for me to deal with my neglect and abuse issues. If you are currently in an abusive relationship, I recommend you go talk to the nearest domestic violence center so they can assist you in planning your exit from the relationship so you can start your healing journey.

I was also grateful to have a workplace that was very supportive of me while I was in the hospital and when I returned to work. The first day back, I received a dozen of roses with a sign that said, "Welcome back!" They never treated me any different than the person they knew before the hospital stay. This made it easy to come back to work.

Identify Your Destructive Patterns—These are behaviors that you repeat that are not good for you but you feel compelled to repeat them. You may or may not be aware of them. For example: I eat large amounts of food and drink 6-10 sodas a day, while under stress. I know that it isn't healthy for me but it helps me cope so I continue the pattern. For three years, I would lose my weight and go from a size 12 to a size 18W. When I did lose weight as people noticed my success, I'd get scared of being hurt again. Then I'd go back to eating and gain the weight back. For some reason I feel safe being overweight. This explains for me why my weight goes up and down. I am still working on this in therapy to find the root from where this belief and trauma comes. It is going to be an ongoing battle but I will accomplish it. What are your destructive patterns? Make a list. Think of behaviors you hate. Those behaviors are…?

Identify Triggers and Your Emotions—It is important to identify your known triggers and to keep track of new ones. Also recognize how you feel while being triggered because if you do you will be able to control your emotions better because you will know where the source is coming from and it won't be so scary when the triggers surface. It also alerts you to go to the coping skills learned to eliminate the trigger and awful emotions before they become out of control and end up in an angry outburst or crying spell. Do something like this—old triggers cause feelings….. and my new triggers are…and cause these feelings….

Coping Skills—This is how you will be able to live your life normally while being able to work and succeed in the workplace, school environment, and everyday life events. With the skills I have learned, I have been able to function at a high capacity and no one knows of my disorders because I function normally. I am now at the point in my healing journey that triggers and anxiety are minimal outside of therapy. Most of my triggers and anxiety come while in my therapist's office when she purposely triggers me to do the therapy treatment she uses to help heal me.

Examples of coping skills are:

Breathing Techniques—Learning to breathe in and out deeply while concentrating on breathing in the positive and letting go of the negative attitude, emotions and images.

Positive Imagery—This can be a CD you buy that guides you to a relaxed state of mind or place. It can also be you guiding yourself to your safe place and spending time with your "child within".

I had fun imagining my child self taking my adult self to the candy store and taking her to my safe place that I had as a child. It took a memory that I used to do alone while feeling sad and turning it around to be a happy positive memory. Turning the memory into something positive helps the "child within" to heal because she no longer feels sad and alone. This is also called repair work.

Talking to the "child within" When Triggered—By talking and connecting to the "child within" you may be able to figure out from where the trigger is coming and resolve it. You need to comfort the "child within" by saying statements to yourself like: "It is okay, little one, the bad people are gone. You are safe. I am here to protect you. You are not alone this time. I am here with you." These statements along with the breathing techniques can calm you down and restore you back to the adult presence rather than staying in the childlike ego-state. If you have time to stay there with your "child within" and take care of her or him for a while this will help her or him to heal. If you are at work or school, calming yourself will help get through the day until you are able to spend time with your child self.

Art Therapy—I had art therapy and it taught me how to play again which was something my "child within" needed to cope. I have done collages by ripping out magazine pictures and letters to develop a picture that tells a story about me, my abuse, what was lacking in my childhood to inspire myself. The themes can be different for each collage. I currently am working on a survival doll that shows all the injuries and trauma my small body suffered and survived.

When I get annoyed or frustrated, it is usually because I have neglected to connect with the "child within" and she feels abandoned and unloved. When this happens, try to do an art project such as a collage, coloring a picture or going outside to play on the swings, anything a child would enjoy doing. You will be amazed that by doing this, it will relieve the negative emotions quickly. There are samples of my collages on my website www.silencednolonger.com under Therapies Received.

Develop a Safe Bag and bring it with you—If I get triggered while spending time with family or out and about, I can take one of my items out of my bag and concentrate on coping and resolving the trigger. The bag is full of items that make me feel safe. My safe bag has my journal, a candle, tea, lotion, reminders from therapy, relaxation CD, positive affirmation cards, and a gem that represents the strength I have inside. Each person will have different items that make them feel safe.

These are just a few of many coping skills. Find the coping skills that work best for you and use them. The questions I would like you to ask yourself are: Do I know the warning signs? Have I told a safe person my warning signs so they can alert me? How can I help myself or others when warning signs start up?

Write your answers down and act on them. Give yourself time. It is not a race. There may be days when you feel you have regressed or lost ground but remember tomorrow is another day. Keep trying because your life is worth reclaiming. If your life isn't worth reclaiming because all you have known is abuse, then this gives you the opportunity to make a new life for yourself.

Part Nine
Author Letter to Readers

Chapter 22
Letter from Author

When I started my healing journey, I was against counseling, psychiatric help and medications. I am continuing my healing journey with acceptance of all the help these services provide. I used to think I was weak to need help but now I know it is the opposite. I am stronger for needing help because I chose to deal with the struggles rather than hide them. I also realized the services provided were my lifeline to a happier, fuller, and renewal of life. I feel reborn because the sky is the limit for me because all the counseling and therapy showed me that I have no limits anymore. I can do anything I put my mind to do. I accept there may be times I go backwards but I proved to myself that I can survive the difficult healing process. I have confidence I can do it again if I ever need to.

I go to my behavior health appointments with no embarrassment or shame, to check on my medications so I stay well. When I go to my appointments, I feel like one of the crowd like Norm on the Cheers television show with the line "Everybody knows your name." The more I go to my appointments the more I recognize the patients and they recognize me.

Feeling open with your caregivers, the office staff, and other patients will become the new normal in your life and will feel good. When patients start to talk to you and share their stories and trust in you, you'll be happy. This is where new friendships are made and true bonds are created because both of you know each other's struggles and accept the other person as they are.

I also enjoy going to my therapy appointments: counseling with Sandy to talk and use the EMDR, brainspotting, positive imagery and resource building therapy and art therapy with Cindy. I enjoy creating beautiful things out of my traumas because it transforms the hurt and pain with understanding and renewal of life. I definitely will continue my therapy because I learn new coping skills, and different ways at looking at life's situations. It helps sustain my healthy mental awareness.

I will probably never be off medications but now I am okay with that because I never want to affect my family in a hurtful way and don't want to take more precious time away from enjoying life with them. I never want to experience the flashbacks, body memories, fear, anxiety, nervousness or turning the abuse on myself or my family ever again.

I am proud to be who I am because I am a SURVIVOR of sexual, physical, and mental abuse and childhood neglect. I am a normal person who is deserving of a good life without anxiety controlling me and my family. I deserve to live freely without worry, fearful thoughts, or sickness from being obese with high blood pressure and cholesterol. I am worth fighting against my hurt self by stopping self-sabotage and becoming a healthier and beautiful me.

Message to my readers:

Flashbacks in Post-Traumatic Stress Disorder: Surviving the Flood took you through my personal healing journey. Your journey will not be exactly the same but by reading about my experiences, struggles, and sharing my coping skills and healing process, I hope that it will inspire you to seek help through the use of medication, counseling, and social services. These are three important ways to help you and your children through the emergency stage of healing and will help you rebuild your family into a healthier, stronger unit. You need to start the healing process TODAY, not tomorrow, next week or a month from now but right now! Reclaim your life and teach your children how to protect themselves when they are not with you so they change the patterns for future generations.

If you think you are not strong enough, I guarantee you are stronger than you think. I fought for myself in the hospital and you will too. I learned there is no shame to ask for help. I had to be admitted in crisis care through the ER of a hospital and no one made me. I admitted myself. I felt in control when everything else seemed out of control. Did you ever hear the phrase "Someone always has it tougher than you do?" Well it's true. I saw a lot of patients who had it a lot harder than me and they kept fighting for themselves so that gave me the strength to do the same.

Don't keep your abuser(s) secrets because it is keeping them out of jail which gives them time to abuse others while you remain sick and trapped. Don't let the *silence* destroy you by turning the abuse inward with self-sabotage, like I did. I was so beat down emotionally that I stopped loving myself and it almost destroyed me and my family.

You are worth putting yourself first by loving yourself, allowing others to love you, and putting a stop to hiding behind the food or alcohol addiction, bulimia, anorexia, or self-mutilation to help numb the pain. This only makes things worse. I used food and soda to numb my pain and now I am five foot two and weigh two hundred fifteen pounds. I have horrible health. I have a lot of work to do to return my body to a healthier state but I am well on my way because my mind and spirit are healing.

If you can't do it for your adult self, do it for your "child within." Remember back to when you were being abused. Being the adult you are now, would you allow it to happen to that child? ***"No, you wouldn't!"*** You would do anything you could to protect her or him. What helped me was to get out photos of all the stages of my abuse from picture albums so that I could see the child that was abused. In this way, I could stop blaming myself. When I looked at the photos, I no longer saw myself. I saw a child that needed protection and that helped me start the healing process.

If you are in doubt of yourself and your memories, don't be. If you are having flashbacks, no matter whether it is your family member, a friend or a stranger, it happened. It is not your fault that this happened to you, nor should you blame yourself. You have a right to live a happy abuse-free life and remember the abuser(s) want you to remain scared so you don't tell.

You are in charge of your way of life, if you don't like it currently then you have the power deep within yourself to change it. The counselors and medications will help you to find your deepest power to help heal your mind, body and spirit. Once that is done, you can accomplish your goals that were put on a shelf for later but later never came. If you want to go back to school, get the dream job or a promotion, or get back into the workforce, you can. You owe it to yourself to take back your dignity, body, emotions, and resolve any shame or feelings of fault from your abuser(s). It will leave them powerless and you, the strong survivor.

I thank you for reading my book, sharing in my experiences while I healed. I hope your expectations were met. God bless and keep you and your family safe!

Leslie Raddatz, Author

Testimonials

From author to Leslie Raddatz—After writing an article for her website <http://homecomingvets.wordpress.com/>

Leslie Raddatz and her father have done something very courageous. They have exposed their frightening worlds both suffering with post-traumatic stress disorder (PTSD).

Returning soldiers feel shame because they've been trained to be tough. They are not cowards. They think they should be able to overcome this on their own. They certainly won't ask for help and let everyone think they are needy. This is why it has been so difficult over the years to get our mentally suffering vets into effective rehabilitation programs for PTSD. Their own military culture shuns them. Veterans Affairs has downplayed the seriousness of PTSD for years by refusing to understand the condition and disallowing veterans' claims, leaving many to a shiftless, homeless life. Even worse, some in utter despair have committed suicide. These tragedies could be overcome if we choose as a society to recognize it and support treatment?

Scientists studying PTSD believe that the brain, when it is subjected to repeated and extended surges of adrenalin, short circuits—like an overloaded socket—or goes into defense mode to protect itself from breakdown. Thus, when episodes are triggered, the brain keeps replaying scenes from the moment the short circuit happened, like a broken record. It simply doesn't know how to repair the fissure in its neural network.

This helps explain why civilians suffer the same "shell-shock" symptoms as soldiers. Trauma that overloads the brain comes in many forms, not just in combat. PTSD is never caused because your character isn't strong enough. No one knows his or her genetic limitation until it happens, and then it is too late. The only way to circumvent this wall of "silent" suffering is to face it and talk about it with others going through the same horror. Talking about it reduces the fear that you are the only one going insane.

In writing her book, *Flashbacks in Post-Traumatic Stress Disorder: Surviving the Flood,* Leslie Raddatz pulls us into her world of nightmares and humiliation. It's not a sob story. It's straight forward talk. She does not want you to feel sorry for her, or her father. She wants you to understand what it is like to live in their shoes. It's also to helps a reader see that anyone can suffer from PTSD, if put under "breaking-point" conditions. There but by the grace of God go I!

By writing about her experiences, Leslie is not just doing an exercise to help her heal. She is inviting her readers to heal with her. She is providing you with an opening conversation with someone living with PTSD. She is also sharing the steps she took to find sanity and serenity.

Bonnie Toews, former journalist, Canada
Canadian Veterans Advocate http://www.homecomingvets.com
Spy Thriller Novelist http://www.bonnietoews.com

Ella Sandwell Radio Interview:
I met Leslie Raddatz while doing an interview with her. I found her information and experiences very compelling. Her book shows her passion, her desire to pass on what she has learned from her experiences, and it tells a story of not only surviving but having the strength to move forward from things in her past with vigor and a strength that is hard to match. With her writing she shows humor, compassion, and a willingness to control her surroundings in spite of what she has been through in a way

that all of us could learn from. I hope you share offering congratulations to Leslie on a wonderful must read book! ~ Ella Sandwell

Facebook https://www.facebook.com/theEllaSandwell
Facebook Fan Page https://www.facebook.com/EllaSandwellsPage
Wildella TOP40 radio www.live365.com/stations/wildella

From Website—www.silencednolonger.com

"My name is Andrea and I'm a survivor of sexual assault. I have PTSD and my psychiatrist recommended Leslie Raddatz and her website to me. She has helped me to understand what is going on with me and ways to cope with it. I'm sure with her website she can help many others as she has helped me. Thank you so much Leslie." Andrea J, Survivor of PTSD, Waupaca, WI

From Blog—www.silencednolonger.blogspot.com

"As a PTSD survivor I recognized myself in many of Leslie's posts and when I read the information on her website I didn't feel as alone as I had before. The information gave me hope and encouraged me to not give up in a time I really needed it. Leslie reached out to me so I could reach out to her. Thank you, Leslie." Andrea W., Survivor of PTSD, Germany

From Website & Blog

Blair Corbett, survivor coach, Founder and Executive Director, Ark of Hope for Children, Inc. www.arkofhopeforchildren.org

Flashbacks in Post-Traumatic Stress Disorder: Surviving the Flood has the ability to help so many, whether dealing with their own PTSD or that of a loved one. The insights shared through Leslie's website and separate blog, *Silenced No Longer* first brought her to my attention. The manner in which she courageously shared her experiences as a child abuse victim and how those experiences drastically altered her adult life are very insightful.

At first I saved some of her blog and website material to assist me as I help victims of child abuse through our non-profit ministry, *Ark of Hope for Children*. Thankfully she allowed me to share her blog posts through Ark of Hope's online daily publication, *Child Abuse Victims Daily* on Paper. li where many more could be touched using her insights.

It became apparent as I came to know Leslie personally that she could be a great advocate for those we had begun helping online. I knew she could, if willing, help facilitate online through the brand new social support network that I had become heavily involved in called *Justice For All Revolution*. Thankfully, my instincts were right on. I have been online with her in the JFAR support chat rooms as she delicately assists other victims as they strive to become strong survivors. I am thrilled to partner with her as she shares the knowledge and coping skills she have mastered, in order to help survivors the world over.

From Facebook

After the testimonial from Andrea W. was published Leslie received this response: "That's why I wanted you to be a friend on my Facebook. After reading your testimonial, it was almost a reading about me. We have so much in common it's unreal!" Sherry, Plant City, Florida

From Twitter- lraddatz1

After Michael read my blog he commented on twitter: "What a life story you have. Sincerely."

Leslie's response: "The only way through all of my life experiences is hard work and transformation from victim to the Ultimate Survivor."

Michael's response: "That is so well stated. I admire you. Cheers Michael." Michael, Author, Sainte-Adele, Canada

Flashbacks in Post-Traumatic Stress Disorder: Surviving the Flood

From Branched Out Social Media

"Leslie is the type of person who makes hard work seem easy. Gets results with ease. Amazing." Dolores, Self Employed Author

From Readers of Completed Manuscript

Flashbacks in Post-Traumatic Stress Disorder: Surviving the Flood was a page turner. I couldn't stop reading it. As I read Leslie's book, I realized how much I could relate to her with the trauma and abuse that she experienced. I, myself, am a survivor of PTSD and spousal abuse. I found this book to be inspirational and a source of healing. I learned more about PTSD and the treatments available through Leslie's eyes as well as finding new hope for my continual healing journey. I know that everyone heals at different times and there will be times survivors will regress but we are further ahead than most. You will never forget your past but your future will be much more manageable and you will be able to enjoy life more fully. It is sad how much Leslie and I had to go through but just knowing that there is help available is comforting and will bring a renewal of hope for the other people that read this book. Lisa, PTSD Survivor, Oshkosh, WI

Blurbs

Story of triumph over adversity, and hope in the midst of horrific flashbacks.

From Barbara Shelton's Blog Interview- five day on-line interview was a lot of fun. Each day, Barbara shared a little more of our interview so the readers wouldn't get overwhelmed with the information.

There were many comments from the readers:

Thank you Barb and Leslie for this great, informative interview. I suffered severe childhood abuse as a child and so much of this is hard for me to read; especially that other women had to suffer as I did. I thought for so many years that I was the only one. I never even told my husband until we had been married for 15 years. It wasn't something that was talked about at all back then. Diana, Child Abuse Survivor

PSTD, a term that I didn't know anything about, but this blog post gives some good and helpful information about this subject. Thanks for giving us this insight. Cecilia, Interested about the subject

Barb thanks so much for alerting me to your blog today. Leslie, it's difficult to know what to say. As one of my characters says to another in my upcoming book, "No one should have to suffer like that from the people who are supposed to love them most." I want to wrap you in my arms and give you a huge hug of Christian love. Truly, the Lord is using you in a mighty way for His glory in sharing your story and giving others hope. Thanks from the bottom of my heart for all you do. Blessings always. JoAnn, Author

Thank you for this emotional, informative and inspiring week of interviews, ladies. I've learned so much about both Leslie and you, too, Barb. I've had tears in my eyes and been moved more than you can know by what I've read here this week. Such a heartbreaking yet incredible story of triumph over adversity, and hope in the midst of sometimes horrific storms. May the Lord bless you, Leslie, and I'll pray with you for Him to open the "right" doors of His choosing in order to prepare your proposal, find and agent and get your story out to the masses. It's well-deserving of being told, and can help so many. Abundant blessings to you, Leslie, and Barb. And a very heartfelt thank you. JoAnn, Author

Leslie: It's really important to talk about PTSD. So many have it and don't know it. You speak very clearly about it. Thanks, Barbara for bringing her to us. Anonymous

Barb, I appreciate your interviewing Leslie on this difficult subject. I am happy to read how Leslie has not only survived but is helping others as well. I look forward to tomorrow's portion of the interview. Anonymous

I can identify with Leslie's situation and am happy to read about the strength she has found to not only survive, but also to help others. *Jeanne*

This was a wonderful interview, Barb and Leslie. I know your book is going to help many people who are suffering from post-traumatic stress disorder. I've heard of this but never really understood it until this interview. My heart goes out to you, Leslie, and all that you have had to endure. May God bless you in finding those who need your help. *Linda*

My heart goes out to you and to your father. My brother in law was sent to Vietnam, also, and he would have terrible dreams and wake up screaming. It was really tough on my sister but she was finally able to help him through it. This sort of thing is so sad. Anonymous

I wanted to wait until the end of this remarkable series to comment. WOW, what a post—shocking, eye-opening and even overwhelming at times and yet I am grateful to God that He is a God of Hope and Healing and begins the process with amazing people like Leslie. I can think of SO many people who would benefit from Leslie's ministry, and I pray God uses her mightily for His Glory AND for much-needed healing for His Body. God bless! And, Barb, THANK YOU for an incredible series! *Julie*

We live in a confusing world and to a child like Leslie Raddatz who wasn't taught the usual right and wrong; childhood became critically diabolical and damaging. Perhaps some readers of this book will not believe as Leslie reveals shocking truths. She skillfully describes her feelings about herself as a child and what was happening to her in the moment to her counselor through sophisticated techniques, Eye Movement Desensitization & Reprocessing (EMDR) and brainspotting. Her story pours forth as she remembers scenes in her childhood, teen years into adulthood.

My reactions came tearfully as I longed to hold this child and sooth her hurts and injustices.

Within her soul, Leslie craved healing from her hurts and was prompted to seek help for herself, her last recourse before the onset of PTSD destroyed what mental and physical strength she had left. Leslie's perception, insight and naïve understanding of her mental disorders caused by childhood abuses, traumatic and dramatic events including sexual abuse, rapes, being bullied, parental inattention, family dysfunction…somehow, by the grace of God, she survived.

Leslie and I became friends when I invited her to my blog to be interviewed about her PTSD, healing and this book, *Flashbacks in Post-Traumatic Stress Disorder: Surviving the Flood.* She supplied enough personal information about her life and the book she was writing that we published the continuing interview for five days. The blog drew positive comments and readers' interest. The interviews provided much awareness information about PTSD, somatization and conversion disorders; as well as her websites where she reaches out to other sufferers and victims of these mental disorders.

An incredible young woman, Leslie has become an activist to help others with PTSD and mental disorders. She has been a reservoir of facts and help to me personally. I am the mother to an adult child with PTSD. I know God brought us together to provide hope to others. Leslie is deeply convicted that God has saved her and taught her what she needed to do with her life at the present time.

Yes, Leslie is a true survivor and because she now loves herself…. she sends her warmth and concern for others through prayers and reaching out. I hope the readers of this book are thanking God for never having gone through such punishment; and for those that have, to realize hope is out there, because a woman like Leslie Raddatz cares. Prepare for New Blessings, Barbara Shelton, Daughter with PTSD, Arlington, TX

From Self Help Author

Janell Moon, Counselor, editor, author of *Stirring the Waters: Writing to Find Your Spirit* (Journey Editions) and ten other books of self-help and poetry. Your warmth comes through as you write and talk about the trauma you endured and the hardship you went through not having an early diagnosis of post-traumatic stress disorder. To share your experience through your book and to be willing to help others who suffer is a lovely experience for me to watch. It is not only your words but your generous heart that will help others. Janell, Counselor, editor, writing coach, author, San Francisco, CA

About the Author

Leslie has lived in Oshkosh, Wisconsin, most of her life. She has three children, two daughters and a son, and is happily married to a supportive man. She has had many traumas and abuse in her life but she also has had many mentors who helped her along the way.

She started working for a fast food restaurant at 16 years old and today she works for an administrative office as an office manager. When she was 18 years old, she became pregnant while still in high school. She was on welfare and received WIC (Women, Infants, Children), Federal help which gave food stamps and a monthly check. She experienced first-hand how people judge and mistreat others in need of help. She dedicated herself to working hard to earn society's respect and to beat the odds again.

Her education includes four degrees: Office Assistant Degree and Administrative Assistant Associate Degree -specializing in software support from a Technical College. She also graduated from the E-Seed program to help her start up her own business. She received *The Achievement Against the Odds* Award in 2002 because three of her instructors nominated her.

She also has a Bachelor of Arts in Business Administration and Bachelor of Arts in Marketing. She accomplished all these degrees while battling with her Post-Traumatic Stress Disorder, conversion and somatization disorders while also raising a family, working and going to night classes full-time.

She has beaten all the odds that were stacked up against her. She is proud to be a Survivor.

Her mission in life now is to help others like her with mental illness and to give them hope, encouragement and inspiration that if she can heal so can they.

Made in the USA
Monee, IL
31 August 2023

41921887R10154